HEALING

Real Stories Told By People Who
Have Overcome The Homeless And
Opioid Epidemics

NELI VAZQUEZ ROWLAND

HEALING

This book is a compilation of stories from people who have contributed a chapter and is designed to provide inspiration to our readers.

It is sold with the understanding that the publisher and the individual authors are not engaged in the rendering of psychological, legal, accounting or other professional advice. The content and views in each chapter are the sole expression and opinion of its author and not necessarily the views of Fig Factor Media, LLC.

For more information, contact:
Fig Factor Media, LLC | www.figfactormedia.com
A Safe Haven Foundation | www.asafehaven.org

Printed in the United States of America

ISBN: 978-1-7342369-9-6
Library of Congress Control Number: 2020922662

This book is dedicated to my husband and co-founder of A Safe Haven, Brian Rowland, and our sons Devin and Dylan.

I'd also like to acknowledge our partners, Mark Mulroe and Sergio Vazquez along with their families for their years of dedication and commitment to our mission.

Special thanks to all the board members of A Safe Haven, our staff members, funders, volunteers, advocates and our families and friends who over the years believed in and never gave up on us, their co-workers, or themselves. They are the real heroes who understood the humanitarian crisis, shared our vision, and did whatever it took to help make it a reality.

Most of all I thank God because we are a testimony that through Him, all things are possible.

TABLE OF CONTENTS

INTRODUCTION

Walking into the lobby of A Safe Haven, you might be greeted by someone like Nina. She's volunteering today at the concierge desk, greeting guests and people in crisis who come to A Safe Haven in Chicago seeking help. Today, she is beautiful, kind, poised, and smart. But not long ago, she shuffled through the doors of A Safe Haven looking beaten and scared, addicted to drugs and alcohol, with her life hanging by a thread.

For over 15 years, her parents tried everything to help Nina break her addictions, from tough love to "club med" type treatment programs. Yet after rehab she would return to their loving care and affluent, Connecticut suburb, only to relapse again. And again. With battered, broken hearts, they looked on helplessly, on edge every time the phone rang and Nina wasn't home, thinking it was the hospital...or worse. Out of desperation and in fear for Nina's life, they searched nationally for something different, something that could reach her, and they found it with A Safe Haven in Chicago. "My parents found me living on the streets and I didn't want to go," recalls Nina, "but they told me I was either going to go there, or to the cemetery. It saved my life."

Today, Nina is successfully working towards self-sufficiency, looking forward to reuniting with her 14-year-old daughter, and well on her way to becoming another A Safe Haven success story. "I have never seen anything like this anywhere in the country. There needs to be one in every city," said Nina. Her story is poignant, and one of more than 130,000 stories from people we have met and whose lives have been transformed since my husband Brian and I were inspired to open A Safe Haven 26 years ago!

After a quarter of a century working on the front lines (and yet in the shadows of the public eye) on behalf of the most stigmatized populations, we are grateful that today our mission and model is being noticed by so many others. As awareness has grown around the issues and populations we represent and the landscape of services available to them is being evaluated and considered, A Safe Haven is frequently lauded by top stakeholders from academia, policy, and public health leaders, businesses and associations, and media outlets and publications as the most vertically-integrated and comprehensive social service, social enterprise, and phased-housing model in the country. We are proud to stand out for our pragmatic approach. Our work is accomplished by engaging like-minded, public and private partners and teams who are committed to helping build and create a model that fosters success and helps lift up the lives of people in crisis into a life of sustainable self-sufficiency. We do it by customizing services and providing the opportunity and resources needed to address and overcome their complex root causes of poverty and homelessness through a holistic and scalable model. Our visible, social, measurable, and tangible economic impact restores lives, unites families, stabilizes neighborhoods, and creates vibrant, viable, and safe communities.

But don't take our word for it. The authors of the stories in this book will tell you how A Safe Haven's forward thinking, multidisciplinary, and holistic approach has helped to release them from the sudden or chronic bondage of homelessness and social and economic crisis while easing their transition into a sustainable, self-sufficient lifestyle. While we bask in the glow of their success, it also saddens us to know that we are simultaneously facing significant pent up and unmet demand for our services because of our capacity restrictions and funding constraints.

It will take more support from additional like-minded leaders from government, the public, businesses, media, and community organizations to make the difference in turning this tide and help build upon a model that is designed to foster success As you read the success stories of the people in this book, know that there is hope and that together we can make a difference with your support of A Safe Haven. Your voice will be needed as we explore the future landscape of potential smart solutions and evidence-based healthcare delivery systems.

When we look into the eyes of people like Nina, we know we are making a difference in her life and the lives of all of those that love and depend on her too. While there are many approaches to helping the homeless, it's good to know that our model of investing in a customized, holistic, fully-developed and comprehensive system that is focused on healing the complex issues of our most vulnerable people, in their time of greatest need, and is committed to opening doors and putting them on a path to jobs and housing. And that offers a priceless payoff for every American!

At a time when the pandemic is predicted to substantially increase the number of homelessness in the world, the social and economic future of generations has never before been more urgent. The good news is that the choice is ours. We urge everyone to get involved, do your homework and help us get this right. Our future depends on us!

Neli Vazquez Rowland
Co-Founder, A Safe Haven
https://www.asafehaven.org
Neli@asafehaven.org
LinkedIn: nelivazquezrowland
Twitter: @neli_rowland

THE STORY OF A SAFE HAVEN

You may wonder how A Safe Haven came to be. Back in the early 90's, I was the mother of a four-year-old boy and pregnant with my second son. Both my husband Brian and I were both financially comfortable after working many years in the financial industry. Being young parents, and first-generation Americans, both Brian and I had overcome personal challenges before achieving financial success, and we were both taught that to whom much is given, much will be required (Luke 12:48). Our parents both lived by that example and were always willing to help those in need. We also wanted to be role models for our children and do something to give back to the community. Coincidentally, it was also a great time to take advantage of a buyers' market in real estate.

The issues of substance abuse and poverty were very near and dear to us. Brian was an army veteran who had struggled with alcoholism in his college years and had been fortunate to be able to get into an exclusive treatment program. It was covered by his medical insurance and he had the ability to pay the high deductible and out-of-pocket expense.

I also appreciated that somehow, I had narrowly escaped my own fate, raised in a tough neighborhood where drug deals, teenage pregnancy, and dropping out of high school were the norm. We intimately understood the magnitude of the social issue and how many lives were lost to the disease of addiction when it was left untreated. So our vision and mission to help people suffering with addiction became personal. Plus, we had the means to help a few people out, so why not do it?

Our goal was to help people in crisis who were struggling with their disease of substance abuse within the existing, completely fragmented, broken and financially unsustainable system. However, we grew frustrated as we searched for an organization to support who had a mission in sync with our own. In our research we found many organizations who were providing a "band-aid" to the needs of those struggling with the disease of substance abuse. Providing shelter was not enough. How can anyone move to self-sufficiency if their underlying co-existing conditions and barriers to a comprehensive range of services and resources are not addressed?

Anyone unable to get access to treatment can lose their job and end up homeless on the street, breaking the law to support their habit. How could they ever recover and break out of the system, without treatment? Substance abuse has no boundaries, but it's true that the majority of those affected were in the poorest populations in our society and lacked the resources, mentorship, and/or access to professional treatment programs, legal representation, bail money, or higher education. They had underlying, systemic issues like poverty, physical and mental health issues, inadequate education and job training, and unemployment that needed to be addressed to change the trajectory of their lives and reverse a cyclical problem which could affect their families for future generations. We did not see such a model available, so this is what we grew at A Safe Haven.

We began by purchasing a distressed, thirteen-unit building near the Logan Square area of Chicago with the intention to rehab it, and allow people suffering from substance abuse addiction to live there for free as they pursued life in recovery. We called the project A Safe Haven.

To fulfill our vision, we needed resources, and banks were not about to lend us money to build housing for recovering addicts, especially when we did not have a baked-in revenue model in our plan. So, we took the personal risk and invested our own money. Later, we invited some investors to help us renovate and build multiple abandoned apartment complexes in distressed communities.

Much to the surprise of our family, friends, and colleagues, we dramatically altered our own lives to pursue a new mission in life. We answered the call and replied, "If not I, then who?" We set out to build a social enterprise model that aligned with our personal values and is truly designed to help people aspire, transform, and sustain their lives as we help them to transition from homelessness to self-sufficiency with pride and purpose.

Today, A Safe Haven has evolved into a growing network of over 40 real estate developments that we either own and/or manage located throughout the Chicagoland area, including a state-of-the-art, 400-bed transitional housing program that doubles as our headquarters. It's located on four acres and boasts impressive grounds courtesy of our landscaping trainees. Because of its modern design, most people mistake it for a beautifully kept, professional office building. As architecturally impressive and award-winning as our developments are, the transformative stories of the people inside them is even more astounding. This book is our way of getting those stories out into the world!

SAVING MONEY AND LIVES

When we started A Safe Haven in 1994, the opioid epidemic was on the rise, and the biggest eye-opener for us was the variety of people it reached. We expected people from the inner city, products of a long family history of addiction, poverty, and incarceration, but we also found many people who had led seemingly "normal" lives before becoming homeless. There were suburban housewives with children, who once had stable lives and a home but through an experience like an accident, surgery, or chronic pain, were prescribed addictive pain relievers that took over their lives. They were veterans, who had served their country, fought bravely, and returned home only to face the overwhelming challenges of finding employment, housing, and dealing with chronic pain which they managed with opioids or alcohol. There were young people, full of potential, who lost an affluent life because of a bad decision that led to a habit and alienated their entire support system. Hopelessly addicted and now homeless, many of our residents had broken the law to support their habit and now had a prison record that kept them from finding employment.

We watched as a failing "War on Drugs" and increased prison capacity became omens that showed that America had lost its way. Like standing in the tracks of an oncoming train, we saw how the growth of an addicted population would derail not only the lives of people, but the financial well-being of all areas of society, including healthcare, educational and criminal justice systems, housing, and unemployment. Today, it is absolutely no surprise to those of us on the front lines that the American prison population makes up 24 percent of the world prison population (ranking us at #1), even though the U.S. makes up only five percent of the world's population.

We helped create licensure for our field and then became the State's first licensed recovery home. We listened and filled in the gaps of our residents' lives, connecting the dots to their self-sufficiency. When we needed funding beyond what the government could provide, private donors and investors stepped in, leading to a practical application of public-private partnerships aligned to meet and leverage our respective resources to achieve our common goals. Today we successfully provide housing and services for about 5,000 homeless people annually.

Once our residents were successfully in recovery and deemed work-ready and stable by a multi-disciplinary team of A Safe Haven professionals, they still had many overwhelming barriers to employment because of their checkered pasts and poor credit history. We needed compassionate employers willing to take a chance on our residents who were solidly ready to return to work and live independently. We wondered, who would hire these people? Then we realized, we could!

We began investing in social enterprises, a business that makes a profit but also provides an added social benefit. We acquired and began growing a landscaping company which offered gainful, meaningful employment to help residents bridge to self-sufficiency. Today, our organizations put about 1,000 people a year to work directly in our A Safe Haven landscaping business, catering business, and through our staffing service company with employers willing to hire people who have earned a second chance.

The final piece of our self-sufficiency puzzle was to provide a phased, real estate development model which now allows people to move seamlessly from transitional, supportive, affordable, senior and veteran housing, based on their unique circumstances. This is one of the most celebrated and exciting steps to self-sufficiency.

JOIN THE MISSION

At A Safe Haven, most of our residents complete our program in months and move on to gainful employment and permanent housing after 90 days. For someone newly released from prison and facing barriers to jobs and housing, A Safe Haven reintegrates them into society with compassion, support for recovery, and the ability to earn a living wage. They prove that the individuals who have once been considered society's "throwaways" can transform into positive, productive members of society with an appropriate program that addresses their complex problems. Brian and I are proud to be recognized by leading academic, public health, public policy and business associations and organizations across the country as the pioneering architects tackling one of America's biggest challenges. A Safe Haven has grown organically, and our response has been innovative, battle-tested and anchored with performance metrics and tens of thousands of anecdotal stories of success.

As homeless encampments seem to be popping up in almost every American city today, it takes more than good intentions and money to solve the problem. The first-hand stories shared throughout the pages of this book illustrate the value of moving folks through a proven model that leads to self-sufficiency instead of perpetuating their cycle in and out of homelessness, emergency rooms, hospitals, or the criminal justice system. We also cut down on the time it takes to solve the problem, because the more time an individual remains without shelter, the higher the price they pay with their own lives. Their own failed health and long-term dependence will typically continue into the next generation.

Recently, we stepped forward as first responders for the homeless during the coronavirus pandemic. Responding to the inability of homeless people to "shelter in place" if they tested positive for COVID-19, we forged a partnership with the City of Chicago and Rush University Medical Center to build the city's first COVID-19 positive Medical Respite Isolation Center (MRIC) in a wing of our facility. The center provides a place for COVID-19 positive, vulnerable populations—either symptomatic or asymptomatic—to safely isolate and receive in-person, telehealth, and behavioral healthcare services, proper nutrition, and other wraparound services. We are proud to have been able to successfully fill another gap in services by providing our most vulnerable people a place of healing and isolation so they do not spread the disease throughout the city or to their loved ones living in the same household.

Our passionate attempts to help influence the national dialogue around the issues we address have not gone unnoticed. We have won many honors and awards for our social and economic innovation, community impact, and humanitarianism, along with invitations to the White House under both the Obama and Trump administrations. While we are grateful for the recognition, we won't rest until we have helped inspire a much more comprehensive approach for addressing the root causes of poverty and homelessness as a public health issue, and standardizing the institutional health to community-based behavioral healthcare delivery system and treating it as a top national priority. Traditionally, America has relied on siloed institutions and an ad hoc and reactive approach to deal with the underlying issues of our most vulnerable.

Thanks to the courageous testimonies of the wonderful authors in this book which credit A Safe Haven for their success, we hope to show the world that our "proof of concept" delivers our promise of a much more individualized approach which consistently produces positive outcomes. We humbly believe A Safe Haven is a scalable model that can and should be expanded into every major metropolitan city in the country. All we need is help to do it from people like you.

Want to learn more? Please connect with us at info@ASafeHaven.org

ASH
Alumni
Stories

SHERESSE WINFORD

"The same things that got me sober will keep me sober."

Graduating Class: 2010
Length of Stay: 8 months
Current Status: Sr. Collection Representative

GOD IS NOT DONE WITH ME YET

I would like to start off by introducing myself. My name is Sheresse Winford and I am a recovering alcoholic and addict. I was born and raised on the west side of Chicago. My mother raised me along with four siblings. As a child, I would spend the summer in Clarksdale, Mississippi with my grandmother. I enjoyed going down south with my family. We would go to church and do other fun activities.

TEENAGE REBELLION

When I became a teenager, I didn't want to go anymore. I wanted to stay in Chicago and hang out with my friends. I became rebellious around the age of 14, shortly after my father died.

I would sneak the alcohol that my mother had in the house to drink with my friends, until she found out that her liquor was missing, and I didn't have access anymore. By this time, I started hanging out with friends and skipping classes, or I didn't go altogether. I eventually dropped out at the end of my sophomore year and I landed a job at McDonald's, which didn't last very long.

By this time, I was getting in trouble at home. My mother would punish me and one day I decided to run away from home so I could finally do what I wanted. My mother and the police came looking for me because I wasn't over the age of 18.

I began drinking on the weekends. This started out as fun. I got myself a fake ID so I could get into clubs and I was hanging in the streets late at night, sometimes until daybreak. I did this for a while until I decided I wanted to go back to school. I chose to go to nursing school, but I quit. Then I tried cosmetology school, but I quit again. I never finished what I started.

This was when the real trouble began. I got caught up with the wrong crowd and started stealing from retail stores. At first, we were stealing the clothes to wear them but then we started selling them to have money for clubs and alcohol. When I went to jail, my mother and my aunt came and got me from the police station.

At the age of 20, I was introduced to heroin. At first it made me sick, but I continued to use it anyway. The drug made me feel, act, and behave differently and I liked it. It gave me the courage to do all of the wrong things. It became a habit, and nobody told me that I would get hooked and become ill when I didn't have it.

THE STRUGGLE

I would stand out on street corners and in neighborhood parks with known gang members and it was only through the grace of God that I didn't end up shot or killed. The streets took me to places that I never thought I would go. I was caught up in the grip of my illness. When I was a child, I never thought that I would travel down this dark, painful, and lonely road. I wanted to be somebody.

I had dreamed of being an attorney and studying law. Instead, I started breaking the law and became a felon with a criminal record of retail theft and drug charges. In the process, I gave birth to five beautiful children. DCFS got involved and my mother was given custody of them. She provided a safe place for my children while I ran around like I didn't have a care in the world.

It made me feel shameful, guilty, and hopeless. I just couldn't stop. I couldn't do it for my kids, my mother, or myself. My disease robbed me of being both a mother and a daughter. I was never available for anything and at family gatherings, I was always missing in action. I told myself that I could stop whenever I wanted and I made several attempts on my own, but nothing worked.

I tried only using on the weekends and that didn't work. I tried only drinking and that didn't work. I tried quitting altogether and I never made it past 60 days. I went to detox, but I didn't stay. When I went to prison, I went to the drug addiction unit and took every class they had on anger management, as well as group therapy and several other self-help groups. And when I got out, I would do the same thing over again. I wouldn't follow the recovery plan they gave me for outpatient treatment. This vicious cycle lasted for over 18 years.

Finally, I grew tired of the way that I was living; life was passing me by. I wanted better for myself. I prayed to God to be free, free from the hell I had made for myself.

The last time I went to jail, I cried out to God that I was sick and miserable. It was different this time. I asked for help. I had heard of places that help people break free of their addictions and I hoped and prayed that it would work for me. I asked the Decatur Correctional Center and they called A Safe Haven for me. They interviewed me over the phone, and I was accepted.

After I was released on parole, I didn't go to my mother's house. I knew that I needed help, so I went straight to A Safe Haven. I wanted to give myself a chance and I believed in my heart that if it worked for so many others. then it would work for me too.

HEALING BEGINS

On October 6, 2009, at the age of 38 my new life began. I was sober for about four months. When I arrived at A Safe Haven, the only thing that I knew was that I didn't want to live the way I was living anymore, so I stayed, listened, and learned how to recover. I was assigned a counselor and she gave me instructions, told me about the rules, and gave me recovery planners, which were so important. I had to log everything I did throughout the week and be responsible. They offered so many groups, meetings, and many other resources. I went to the clinic to get a physical and I learned how to start taking care of myself mentally and physically. I never wanted to listen to anybody or follow any rules or laws. I was always breaking them, but I knew that in order for this to work I had to change my way of thinking. My mindset changed from negative to positive. I became willing to do whatever it took to change my life, so I followed the rules. I didn't want to become homeless again.

Each day I got up early in the morning and made my bed, did my chores, went to group meetings, and met with my team lead once a week. When my first 30 days were up, I was sent to an outside Alcohol Anonymous meeting and that was the best thing that could have ever happened in my life. They sent us out to those meetings whether we wanted to go or not. I attended religiously. In rain, sleet, or snow, I went. I met a lot of different people and built a foundation with new friends.

I knew I couldn't stay forever, and I wanted to find a job, so I went to a computer class to learn how to write a resume and I began looking for work. This wasn't an easy task for me. I had a criminal background and I was rejected many times, but I didn't give up. It took five months before I got a yes and this was through the earn fare program at the Illinois Department of Human Services, a program that helps adults become self-sufficient and gain working experience.

I didn't have to pay to stay at A Safe Haven and I thank God for that because I was unable to pay. I didn't have anything except clothes, so I worked and saved my money until I bought furniture, found a place, and moved out. I didn't want to move out west. I wanted to stay connected, so I found a place within walking distance of A Safe Haven. I continued to attend picnics and other activities there. I was later asked to chair the AA meetings on the weekend, and I did this for seven years. I wanted to give back what was so freely given to me.

I'm so grateful for that service work because I was a loner who lacked communication skills. The responsibility helped me learn to interact with other people I didn't know. I went to different meetings and introduced myself to someone who I would encourage to share their experiences, strength, and hope with the residents.

I met so many different people and some of them would ask me to come out and speak at the meetings they were chairing. I didn't know it at the time, but I was building character, and this enhanced my self-esteem. I no longer felt like a shy little girl. Because I stayed connected, I was given information that helped me get my criminal background sealed and expunged. I also got my driver's license.

I am grateful for my journey. I love myself today and because of that, I am able to love other people. I have been sober for over ten years and I could have never done this by myself. Today I am gainfully employed, responsible, and I continue to help others. I am still an active member of AA. I have a sponsor and I continue to ask for help. I don't ever want to think that I can live in recovery by myself. I attend three or four meetings a week and I stay connected with the fellowship.

I am also a church member. I love God and all of the things he has done in my life. I no longer look back at the person I used to be. I love my life right now. I still face challenges in life, but I don't give up and throw in the towel.

I am full of ambition with hopes, dreams, and goals to build a better life for myself. I would like to say that my journey has been easy, but it hasn't been. I have to continue to put in the work. The same things that got me sober will keep me sober. I trust this process and the gift that I was given from God.

I no longer take my life for granted. I thank God every day when I wake up in the morning and before I go to bed at night. I like the person that I see when I look in the mirror. I can smile again, and I feel happy, joyous and free on the inside. My children are all developing into young men and women and my prayer for them is that they have healthy, successful, and prosperous lives and never take the path I did. I thank God for direction as I work the twelve steps of AA with my sponsor and practice the principles in all my affairs. I live and enjoy life one day at a time. I'm not perfect, but I thank God for showing me grace and mercy. I am so very grateful that I'm not where I used to be.

FINAL THOUGHTS

To me, homelessness does not happen overnight. Many events take place before it happens. Lack of education, drug and alcohol addition, unemployment, affordable housing, and mental illness are all issues that need to be addressed to have fewer homeless people in our country. Reducing homelessness would reduce criminal activities and overcrowding of people in the jails and prison systems who have underlying issues.

I believe that building more places like A Safe Haven, which end homelessness and help individuals with the issues that accompany homelessness, can put others on the road to recovery so they can live healthy lives. I also hope for:

- More housing to help low income and below poverty level people have a safe place to stay once they leave a recovery setting or shelter.

- Offer more jobs with on-the-job training for people with little education.
- Offer more funding to all recovery homes and shelters to support recovery times longer than three or six months. Some people need that long to heal.
- Have more counseling centers treat mental illnesses, which is real in our country. Beyond getting a job and housing, people need treatment for mental illness.

After 18 years of heroin addiction and bouts of incarceration, Sheresse now lives soberly and works in the collection industry, where she has received several awards for being employee of the month.

HEATHER BRAHOS

"Can you imagine not having a place to lay your head?"

Graduating Class: 2013
Length of Stay: 6 months
Current Status: Sales Manager

SAVING MY LIFE

It was a cold day when my mother left my father. He didn't want her to go, but he was a man who required a submissive wife, and my mother was a stubborn woman. He still loved her with his whole heart. She pushed me away in a stroller with only a bucket of quarters to her name. I'm not quite sure if she even had a destination, but I would like to believe that her intentions were good. She raised me alone while battling demons that would eventually take her life and send me down my own path of destruction that almost claimed mine as well.

INFLUENCES OF YOUTH

As a child, I remember my mom bringing me into bars that I should not have been in, stepping over her wherever she had passed out, and vodka bottles hidden everywhere. I may have been in fifth grade when she did her first stint in rehab. I didn't understand it at all, but I remember her being better after that.

In sixth grade, I met a girl, rest her soul, who had a different struggle while growing up. She introduced me to gangs, drug dealers, drugs, and late nights by the beach. *This is my life*, I thought.

The summer before seventh grade and starting at a new school, my mother caught me sneaking a boy into my house. She had her first drink in two years that day. She also called my father and expressed to him that she thought it would be better if I went to live with him. When he took on the task, he didn't know me well, so I took advantage of the situation.

During my freshman year, my mother and father decided that they would try again, for my sake. In my sophomore year we moved to a house in the suburbs and I transferred schools. I got invited to my first party, and I was consumed. I attended the best parties with the coolest kids and the best drugs around—ecstasy, acid, cocaine, you name it. Heroin, otherwise known as blow, came into the picture and it never crossed my mind that this drug was any different from the rest. I didn't know it would change my life and all of the lives of the people who loved me.

I had no idea what I was in for as I sat in the police station bathroom getting high after my father caught me stealing. I was 17 now and facing a Class X felony charge with possession in a penal institution. After twenty-four hours, the withdrawal sickness had consumed me. I called my mom and my dad and told them I had been assaulted and they must come and save me. *It's jail,* I thought. *Of course they will come and get me.*

My dad called the jail to make sure he could bail me out and the officer asked, "May I ask why you want to pick her up?" My father told him about the assault and the officer told him it was a lie. Nobody came to get me and now I had caught my second case while in custody—obstruction of justice. I don't remember how many days or weeks I sat in that holding cell. Everything was taken from me, including my clothes. I was put on suicide watch and the officers absolutely hated me. My soul fell apart in that time, along with my body, and my will to live.

TRAGIC TURN

After a month, I was released. My mother was now living with my grandmother in Chicago and that was where I went. We were supposed to be each other's strength and purpose for wanting to do better, but it was so hard. I moved to a halfway house where she volunteered her time, and I started Narcotics Anonymous (NA) meetings for the youth. I was chairing my first meeting, after relapsing only an hour prior, and my father was standing at the glass door. He motioned for me to come out, and he told me that a warrant had been issued for my arrest for the charge of possession in a penal institution. I was in trouble again. My mom arrived shortly after my dad to tell me that she loved me and to take my belongings. She was drunk again. I found myself in the back of my dad's car, on the way to jail, again.

This time was different. All of the officers knew me and said that my previous visit had made them change all of their intake procedures. That was the first time I was threatened by an officer. I remember wondering if they were allowed to do that. I was only there for a week when they popped open my door and said to pack up. I was ecstatic to be out as my dad drove us home and I didn't ask any questions. When we got home, I immediately went to wash the "jail" off me and he called my name in a strange way that I didn't recognize. I went downstairs and that was the moment my entire world fell apart. Through streaming tears, he was able to choke out, "Mommy died."

I left shortly after that, with only the clothes on my back and no money to my name. My mom had supposedly killed herself and it was my fault. Everyone knew it. I had no idea where I was going or where I would end up. I just kept walking down the road. I spent my eighteenth birthday homeless in a park. That was where I slept and kept my belongings; my neighbors were a family of raccoons. Can you imagine not having a place to lay your head?

I was still a junkie with the urge to numb my pain. I would walk and beg for change until I had what I needed to be comfortable, just to do it all again the next day. This went on for three years. I slept in gangways, people's cars, stairwells, trains, and garages. I ran from the law, I ran from my family, and most of all, I ran from myself.

Eventually my past caught up with me, along with seven warrants, and I went to prison. When it was time for parole, my father allowed me to come home. It was right before my twenty-first birthday, and I was well. I got a job, bought a car, met a boy, met two boys, and I started doing cocaine again. I awoke the beast and it was only a matter of time before I needed to feed it.

I was working two jobs and making good money, and all the while I was getting high. It seemed to me that nobody knew, but I guess I was wrong. I lost my job because the family found out I was stealing. My dad was so disappointed. I broke his heart, again.

I found a new opportunity at the methadone clinic. The girls and I started soliciting sex and I was in charge. I gave them a place to stay, food, booked their appointments, and drove them to and from their jobs. Sex always sells.

Eventually I lost my car and the roof over my head. You would think I'd be used to it by now. I met a boy and fell in love. It was a toxic love and did more damage than good. I would end up in prison again, only to be released on my golden birthday, the year I turned 27. That is the year I would become pregnant with my son. He is the angel that God sent to save my soul. I got clean on October 11, 2012 at a large treatment center. I completed detox, inpatient, outpatient, family recovery, and family enrichment and got a job again.

TURNED AROUND

When my time was up, I once again had nowhere to go until my counselor recommended A Safe Haven. I would still be able to work and attend meetings. They provided me with a counselor and helped me continue learning how to be a parent. I met some of the finest mentors a girl could ever need at these establishments.

I completed my time at A Safe Haven at almost a year and a half clean. I moved on to live with a friend's mother and an amazing boy I met whose love was not toxic. I worked my butt off that summer so that I could have my very first home—a place that was mine, for my family, where nobody could tell us what to do. I remember handing over the security deposit and first month's rent, furniture shopping, and color coordinating pictures with pillows. This was the life I never dreamed of achieving. It was something so simple and common, but it seemed so out of reach prior to getting clean.

Seven and a half years later, I have truly come a long way. I'm like a regular person now—a productive member of society. I have worked for the same company for six years and I haven't stolen a dime. I got married to a man who loves me for all my scars and sins. We had another baby. Together, we own some property, and our vehicle has full coverage insurance. We have a bank account and a savings account. We have a church that we call our home. I work out early in the morning before work and try to eat healthy during the day. Oh, and my credit score is even high. It's crazy to think I'm just another junkie. I'm so grateful today. I'm grateful just for life itself and my family—I would literally be nothing without them, and the help I got at A Safe Haven. To my older son, thank you for saving mommy's life.

FINAL THOUGHTS

Unfortunately, homelessness in this country is all too common, but a number of different things can be done to prevent it. Awareness is first. Not enough people in power know what is happening in our troubled communities and why. Our veterans are not being treated with the same dignity with which they served our flag, and homeless fathers with children do not have anywhere to go where they can be with their child. If enough of the "right" people knew, I have no doubt a change would be inevitable.

For the people of power, where are you? Many of you do not address this topic because it's not personal for you. Can you put yourself or a loved one in the shoes of a man, woman, or child who is homeless? Can you imagine not having a place to lie your head? Only when you consider all the circumstances that contribute to homelessness—addiction, abuse, mental illnesses, poor communities, lack of education, loss of job, no support system and simply being scared to ask for help—can you start to end homelessness.

If you are interested in reducing the number of people who suffer from homelessness, find ways to help. Spread the word and inform people on the statistics surrounding homelessness. Volunteer at your local shelter, donate clothes and shoes, or participate in a food drive and contribute what you can. Be a face that the homeless community can trust. You just might be the one to save them.

Heather lived through years of substance abuse and life on the streets, before finding A Safe Haven and recovering her life. She is now a stay-at-home mom raising two beautiful boys.

HOPE LARKIN

"A Safe Haven gave me my dignity back."

Graduating Class: 2012
Length of Stay: 8 months
Current Status: In-house Accountant in the Restoration Industry

FROM THE GOLD COAST TO THE GHETTO

Nobody who knew me before 1997 would have ever imagined I would end up a homeless drug addict and in prison. I come from a very stable, upper middle-class family, with a hard-working father who supported his wife and three children and a mother who stayed home full time to take care of our family. There was never any alcoholism or abuse of any kind, and there was never any indication that my life would take such a drastic turn for the worse.

DRUGS & ALCOHOL

Growing up, I was the "golden child". I was an honors student in both grade school and high school. I graduated in the top 2% of my class, and I was a school leader. I was president of my sophomore class and on student executive board my junior and senior years. I was also elected to Homecoming Queen's Court my senior year. In college, I was president of both my sorority and the largest student social organization on campus. I graduated college and started a career at 22 years old at the Chicago Board of Trade. By the time I was 25, I was living in a luxury high-rise on the Chicago Gold Coast.

I had always been a drinker. I had my first drink at 14, drank regularly at 16, and by the time I was 20, I was an alcoholic. At 19, I blacked out at the wheel going 80 mph on the expressway and crashed my car into a cement underpass wall. It was a miracle I didn't kill myself or anyone else. I should have died in that accident.

I was a blackout drinker. I would blackout and wake up somewhere without knowing where I was, how I got there, or what happened the night before.

For 21 years, I drank alcoholically and suffered severe consequences for it; losing jobs, apartments, my driver's license, friends, and even my own family. However, it never occurred to me that the problem was *me*. I blamed my problems and misfortunes on other people and other things, including my family, friends and the world around me.

The beginning of the end happened in 1994 when I was introduced to cocaine by friends. It started out as a weekend thing and then quickly became an everyday habit. In 1996, after I was introduced to crack cocaine, my downfall was swift and drastic. Within nine months I had spent all of my money and had sold everything I owned of value to support my habit. I came home one morning after a 3-day binge to find my worthless belongings on the curb and the Sheriff in my home, evicting me. In March of 1997, I became homeless for the first time in my life.

ON THE STREET

I was terrified when I saw the Sheriff, but as an addict, I went right back to the crack house I had just come from with no thought of my irreplaceable personal items and heirlooms, nor of my two cats and my dog. To this day, my abandoned cats and my dog still haunt me. I was the only mom they had ever known, and I left them heartbroken, homeless, scared, and bewildered. The sheriff took my dog away and I was told they put my 7-year-old house cats in the alley behind my house which, for them, was a death sentence. This is the one heartbreak that all my years of sobriety has not completely healed.

After I became homeless, I bounced from place to place staying wherever I could. There were times I had nowhere to stay. I slept in abandoned buildings, under porches, in alleys, once in someone's tree house in their backyard, and even a port-a-potty. I was out on the streets of Chicago in February. I stole food and alcohol from stores and clothes from thrift shops. I roamed the streets day and night looking for my next high. I lived to use and used to live. My family didn't even know if I was alive or dead. I hadn't spoken to them in a year. I lived through what we call, "pitiful and incomprehensible demoralization."

In 2002, after forging checks to get money for crack, I got caught and went to Cook County Jail for the first time. I went to drug court and told Judge Fox I was an addict and needed help. I received 90 days in a well-known drug rehab center in the Cook County Department of Corrections (CCDOC) and then received probation. I failed miserably. I couldn't stay sober and kept violating my probation.

On probation, I did Sheriff's Furlough and an Intensive Outpatient Program (IOP) and I still couldn't stay sober. I went back to CCDOC another three times for violating my probation and the fourth time, my judge told me he would send me to prison if I violated again. Even with the threat of prison, I couldn't stay sober.

The end finally came on September 14, 2002 when I got caught by the police leaving Cabrini Green at two o'clock in the morning after having bought two dime bags of crack. This is where my addiction had led me, all the way from the Gold Coast to the Ghetto.

Ironically, that night as I was walking to Cabrini Green, I had looked up at the sky and said, "God, please help me. I know what I'm doing is wrong and I can't stop." God's answer to my prayer was to have a police officer tackle me to the ground like a football player and his partner tell me I was busted.

Judge Fox revoked my probation and sentenced me to three years in prison. I returned to CCDOC for the 5th time and served 3.5 months before being sent downstate to serve 7.5 months in prison. I was in the drug rehab unit the whole time, and my job there was to teach adult women how to read and write. I was released early for good behavior but needed somewhere to live or they would have kept me past my release date.

LIFE TRANSFORMATION

The prison social worker found this place called, "A Safe Haven" in Chicago, a recovery home with a specific program for IDOC parolees. I did a phone screening with Belinda K., who had one of the most soothing voices I had ever heard. She said I could come there without any money or insurance, so I agreed. On 7-28-2005, I left prison with nothing other than the charity clothes on my back and a small cardboard box of my meager possessions.

On the train back to the city, I was thinking of all the foods I wanted to eat, all the places I wanted to go, and the people I wanted to see. I was in for a rude awakening. When I got to A Safe Haven, Rosa F. told me all the rules of the facility, including "no movement for 90 days." I wanted to run, but my parole officer told me that if I didn't want to go back to prison, I needed to stay there. Rosa told me that if I wanted to stay there, I needed to follow the rules.

A Safe Haven gave me my dignity back. They taught me how to live again. I had an apartment with three roommates, my own bed, a hot shower, clothes, and a laundry room to wash my clothes, food, and shared responsibilities. I hadn't had any of those things in the two years I was on the streets. Every night I had to wash the floors in the building. It made me feel good when my chore passed inspection by the staff. Something so small made me feel worthwhile again. We did Recovery Education and Life Skills classes every week. We had to make our beds every morning, wash our dishes, and clean our apartment every day. Every day I passed apartment inspection, and that made me feel good about myself.

They also made recovery fun. We had dances, talent shows, picnics, and we went out to eat after meetings and had outing events. They made me understand that being sober could be fun, and that was crucial to my sobriety.

The most important thing ASH did for me was introduce me to Alcoholics Anonymous (AA). They made us go to a meeting every single day. This is where I started hearing other people just like me tell my story and then tell me how they got and stayed sober through the program. For the first time ever, I felt a connection and an acceptance that I had never felt before. AA worked where every rehab I was ever in had failed. These were my people, and I had found my solution. AA taught me how to live life on life's terms without the use of alcohol and drugs. AA changed my life. I completely embraced this simple program and have been sober ever since. I have been completely immersed in AA for 15 years.

There are no words to describe the enormous impact A Safe Haven has had on my life. I would not be where I am today without them. So many people at ASH bent over backwards to help me stay sober. In particular, Rosa Flores, Kim Hill-Bey, Skip Land, Sterling G., and Tom Zastro. These people built me up. They encouraged me, they inspired me, they were hard on me when I needed it, and they kept pushing me forward. I wanted to be just like them and I followed their leads.

In 2006, after a year of being a resident, A Safe Haven hired me as a staff member. This was a pivotal turning point for me. I was able to get back into a work routine with job responsibilities. This job opened doors for me that I never thought would open for me again.

I resigned from A Safe Haven in 2007 to pursue another job opportunity, and my life has continually improved because of all they taught and did for me. I have been continuously employed since I left A Safe Haven and have progressed in responsibility and salary with each new position. I went to prison for check forgery in 2004 and I have been an in-house accountant since 2008. I write checks every day, all day. That is the miracle of what A Safe Haven did for me. It's like Skip always said, "I went from the outhouse to the White House".

My family and I have long since repaired our relationships. Today, it's as if all of my troubles never happened. We have the best times together, and I can be there for them. I have 12 nieces and nephews who have never seen me take a drink. I am making "living amends" to my formerly abandoned cats and dog by being a great mom to my two cats for the past 13 years and my dog for the past eight years. I also volunteer at my local animal shelter, taking care of homeless cats and dogs, as I hope someone else did for my poor animals back then.

I will never be able to repay A Safe Haven, or Neli and Brian, for changing my life. I would certainly be dead if it had not been for their wonderful programs. I wouldn't be where I am today in my career had they not given me that first job. I even met my husband through A Safe Haven in 2006. We've been married since 2008 and he himself is an A Safe Haven success story who owns his own landscaping company. Nothing in our lives today would be possible without A Safe Haven, and for that, A Safe Haven will always have our undying gratitude.

FINAL THOUGHTS

In order to prevent homelessness, we need more "A Safe Havens" in the world. We need more places and programs that can substantially change the lives of other people the way A Safe Haven has changed mine. We need more resources for addicts and alcoholics who suffer. We need more government funding for A Safe Haven and other places like it. We need to educate the public on the fact that addiction is a disease that makes people do things they normally would never do. We need to eliminate the social stigma surrounding addiction and homelessness.

My advice to government policy holders and community leaders would be to consider increasing funding for places like A Safe Haven, who are on the frontlines combating homelessness every day. We need to make the investment in our citizens and our communities for our current, and future, stability.

The best thing that you, the reader, can do is to educate yourself on addiction and homelessness. Forgo the stigma associated with both. Find compassion in your hearts for those who suffer. Call your government officials, write letters and send emails demanding that places like A Safe Haven be funded with the money they need to help others.

Hope Larkin went from living a comfortable life working at the Chicago Board of Trade to decades of substance abuse, incarceration, and living on the streets. Today she lives in sobriety, works as an in-house accountant and has been a sober, employed, homeowner for more than 15 years.

DANIEL RUBIN

"Never quit before the miracle happens."

Graduating Class: 2005
Length of Stay: 5 months
Current Status: Award Winning Hairstylist

THE GIFT OF DESPERATION

On June 1, 2005 I was given the gift of desperation and could admit complete defeat. I am still powerless, but I am not hopeless. I am a recovering crystal meth addict and an alcoholic. I later came to understand that this meant I had to follow simple suggestions. Fifteen years ago, I was broken in so many ways, from being completely miserable to having no life or job skills outside of dealing and using drugs. However, it was all supposed to happen.

SEEING THINGS DIFFERENTLY

I grew up in northwest Evanston and was raised by a loving mother and father. As the older problem child, I took up most of the oxygen in the house. My brother and I fought like animals, but we have always loved each other. I was a tall order from the start. From behavioral issues at school to learning disabilities, I kept everyone on their toes. I knew from an early age how to manipulate people to get the result or outcome I wanted, but it didn't always work in my favor. Often the unexpected happened, and many lost trust in me or wouldn't believe what I said. This was my addict/alcoholic brain working in its pure form before drugs or alcohol ever entered my body.

I can remember feeling different as far back as preschool. I thought that being different was a disability, but I came to understand it as an asset, especially when I was completely honest, which I rarely was. I remember being a child with an intense imagination. I believed that the gingerbread man was real. I thought that the tooth fairy actually came to reward me while I was asleep, and I even went as far as to painfully pull-out baby teeth on my own, because I knew I would get more than five dollars to spend immediately at the five and dime.

For a long time, I thought that the world and universe I had been born into was an alternate reality. I thought that my parents weren't really my parents and that this thing called life and childhood were all part of an elaborate play or virtual game controlled by aliens, or that I was in a very long dream in someone else's mind. Though I felt like it was a boring choice, I was the star, and everything was being done and chosen for me. I felt this way until high school, when I realized that this alternate universe that I thought was real was simply another fantasy created by my untreated addiction.

I was an average student who would take on projects but never complete them. I didn't enjoy traditional forms of academic learning, yet somehow succeeded. I realized at an early age I had an attraction to men, but I didn't know I was gay. I had a secret, a secret which no one could ever find out. If they did, I would have to die, or I would end up with AIDS. This was the extent of what I knew from gay people I had known. I decided I would rather be a secret until my last day on this planet, than be more of an outcast than I already was.

IN SEARCH OF A SOULMATE

The gay thing started to become more concrete. I tried kissing two separate girls when I was young, and I felt nothing. I remember thinking, *Wow, kissing girls is awful. Men have so much more passion and strength.* Not to sound like men do it better, but for me they did, and still do. But every time I got aroused or engaged in anything gay, I felt a deep sense of pain, guilt, and remorse. It was almost the same feeling I had toward the end of my using, but I didn't know the two would have a direct correlation with each other. Thus, I began to hide my true identity and wear a mask. I would go to school and dress like a goth kid in the day and sneak out wearing tight clothes and talking to random men on America Online at night. This carried on from ages 14-19.

I recall the first time I did meth. I was doing my normal weekend routine with my best friend from high school. We had fake IDs and would go to the gay bars in Chicago. One night we were walking the streets of Boys Town when a hot man on a motorcycle pulled up. We chatted and ten minutes later I told my friend I was leaving to hang out with this new beau. He told me everything a young Leo like myself wanted to hear: how good looking I was, how sexy my voice was, how my height and body were god-like perfection. I didn't care that he lived in a weird loft with 15 other artists. I didn't bother to ask him or anyone his age. I just heard what I wanted, and I created a new universe that included him. We hung out in his bedroom and he offered me a line of something. By this time, I had already tried ecstasy and cocaine a couple times. I asked what it was, but he did not outright tell me but said I would really like it. I did it and immediately after, I needed to know what it was. Not because I was afraid, but because it gave me exactly what I wanted in less than ten seconds. My inhibitions, fear, sadness, and not feeling sexy all melted away.

He told me it was crystal and I couldn't believe it. I had been warned for a long time that crystal was the "devil" in drug form, and I had steered clear of it until then. I said, *Great, I need to do this again,* but in my mind I told myself that I needed to do this for the rest of my life.

I was nineteen then and I didn't stop using until June 1, 2005. With my drug of choice in hand and a life full of lies, deceit, and manipulation, I was ready to conquer the world. I had arrived and no one or nothing would ever come between me and crystal. We were soulmates destined for success, fun, and a gateway into acceptance and fearlessness. Boys Town look out. Daniel and crystal were here to stay.

I did everything from selling my body to men for drugs and money all the way to ordering meth in the mail from LA and having my parents receive it from FedEx at their home. I lost all moral or ethical beliefs and created a new alternate universe fueled by meth and devoid of any kind of rational thinking. I was the all-in type of user. Meth was my maker, and I was not ashamed to feel content with doing it for the rest of my life. I never thought I would end up with holes in my face, severe dental problems, catching class X felonies, and the list goes on.

HELP FROM OTHERS

I thought that crystal meth was my wife for life. However, after the third year of using, I wanted a divorce. What she didn't tell me was that she wasn't leaving without a fight. I couldn't stop on my own and in May of 2005, I put myself into the Highland Park Psychiatric Hospital for the sixth time. At the end of my stay, I received a classic intervention from the staff and my parents. I was left with a choice to continue to use and lose all connection with my family or go to treatment. With little drug money left and no friends or job, I threw up my hands and opted for residential treatment.

I could not get sober by just going to meetings and getting a sponsor. I needed a place to go where I could rest. At the height of my addiction, I would stay up for weeks at a time with no sleep. My memories of treatment were taking a lot of naps. I left treatment five months in, but my family wouldn't allow me back home. They gave me a list of sober living facilities and A Safe Haven, which was also linked with the PRIDE Institute of Chicago at the time, allowed me to qualify and take up residence.

At the time, the house I lived in was at Fullerton and Hamlin on the west side of Chicago. I remember hauling my two trash bags full of clothes to the house. It was all I had. I can recall having a meeting sheet, being drug tested randomly, and having regular house meetings and chores to fulfill. I had been so broken from my use and disconnected from the world that I forgot how to live and take care of myself. A Safe Haven helped my early recovery in many profound ways by giving me safe, sober housing, food, and a supportive environment.

From June 1, 2005 to the present, I have maintained continuous sobriety. Recovery and sobriety are the most important parts of my life today. I love going to meetings and being able to tell my story in different ways and through various mediums, such as this one.

When I got sober, I only knew how to use and sell drugs. I had to either go back to school, but I was also a convicted felon. My mom had suggested going to beauty school. I had surrendered thus far, so I was open to anything. I enrolled, and 14 years later, I have a thriving career I never could have fathomed. Not only have I done presentations around the world and won multiple international awards for hair styling and color, but I have a job that brings me joy by helping other people discover and find their beauty (even if it is only skin deep). I own my own home and car, and the "things" in my life are just that—things.

I talked earlier about assets and liabilities. Through working the 12 steps multiple times in recovery, I have come to understand that without this ying and yang, I cannot grow. Without the cloud of drugs, I have to feel life on life's terms. Every day I choose not to pick up drugs or alcohol is a miracle. The steps have given me a new way to navigate my life. I try and practice these principles in all my affairs. Some days I do better than others.

I also discovered that the scheming, manipulative, and impulsive tendencies I had before and during my active addiction can be flipped into behaviors that serve the life path I walk today. I need to be able to convince people of ventures I set out to achieve. I also need to do what is uncomfortable and put myself and my work out for the world to see. I also go to bat for others who are newly sober or who need a chance with work or a nudge toward social engagement. These are some of the ways I can redirect the liability parts of my old lifestyle and change them into assets.

My priceless gratitude comes from carrying the message of recovery for the sick and suffering addict. Today I am not only sponsored, but I also sponsor five other people in recovery. I am also a board member for a nonprofit, youth housing organization for at-risk LGBTQ+ or homeless youth.

I was blessed with the gift of desperation and hopelessness fifteen years ago, but today I am not hopeless or desperate anymore. I continue to have abundance every day in my recovery and I have become more enthusiastic about the life that I thought wasn't real. I sometimes still wonder if my alternate universe idea isn't too far-fetched. The difference today is that I am not a little boy anymore, and I know many others like me.

FINAL THOUGHTS

My final thoughts to anyone new or struggling is to never quit before the miracle happens. Give yourself a chance to live. So many of our problems come from a disease of perception. I have seen and heard it all in the rooms of recovery over the years, but the common denominator from anyone I know with a substance abuse problem is believing you are not worthy or believing that someone else did this to me. Honesty, open-mindedness, and willingness can come from the most hopeless and desperate addict if they are ready to get honest and work to let others love them until they can love themselves.

Homelessness should be eradicated. Addicts shouldn't be criminalized but treated as what we are—sick. If you are reading this with an outsider lens, the best thing you can do is to activate grassroots efforts in your community through volunteering and writing to your local, state, and federal representatives that more support and funding is needed. Finally, remember that if you are struggling, chances are the person you resent the most is also struggling as well. Always practice kindness, especially with those who are sick and suffering.

Most of all, don't quit before the miracle happens.

Daniel Rubin spent years enslaved by crystal meth until he found recovery through A Safe Haven. Today he is an award-winning hairdresser in Chicago and a member of the North American Goldwell Artistic Team.

WILBERT LEE

"If you give love, you will receive love."

Graduating Class: 2012
Length of Stay: 9 months
Current Status: Security Receptionist and Driver

MR. GRATEFUL

My name is Wilbert Lee and I'm a grateful alumnus of the A Safe Haven program. I grew up in the Ida B. Wells housing projects on the south side of Chicago. I come from a big family of 12 children— six boys, and six girls, and I am the youngest boy. My father passed when I was two years old and I grew up in a house where my brothers used alcohol and drugs. In general, I grew up and ended up in a life of violence and uncertainty, since that was pretty much all I knew.

My brothers sold drugs too and as the youngest, they were not the best examples for me. By the time I was in sixth grade, I was selling heroin with them. And then in tenth grade, I tried it myself and fell in love with the way heroin made me feel.

I graduated from Wendell Phillips Academy High School and even enrolled at Kennedy Community College to learn to become a printer. But by then, my addiction to heroin had taken root in my life and would hold me captive for the next 35 years. School became a distant memory as my love of the gangster lifestyle with lots of fast money, drugs, and women took over my existence. I eventually left school; I didn't need it. But it always bothered me that I didn't finish.

Because of my drug use and dealing, I ended up being shot six times. Five of the times occurred within a single year. Then two years later, I got shot again. It was the last straw. It took all of that violence for me to realize, finally, that if I continued my life as it was, I would surely end up dead. In fact, I realized that I was lucky to be alive then, just as I am now. So, I decided to take steps to begin my recovery from my heroin addiction.

A SAFE HAVEN OR BUST

I heard about a recovery home in Kankakee, Illinois from my friends and I traveled there to begin my recovery in 2010. It was a short-term recovery home, so I was allowed to stay there for six months. The program was designed for people in the beginning stages of recovery. I spent most of my time in meetings learning how to remain sober and I had a case manager to support me. But as my six months were coming to an end and I had to plan my next move, I heard about A Safe Haven and it sounded like the program was definitely for me. I wanted to go somewhere I could not only stay in recovery but build a new life for myself with a job and housing.

I called every day, asking them for space and they were always full. I called the next week and the woman on the end of the line said the same thing. No beds. I called the following week, and the following week, always discouraged with the news that the shelter was full. No beds available. But I wouldn't give up. I was bound and determined to get admitted.

Then, in 2011, still without a notion of whether or not they would be able to accommodate me, I took a leap of faith and hopped a bus to Chicago. I arrived homeless and made my way to the door of A Safe Haven. I was crying crocodile tears, asking the person at the front desk to take me in. They weren't quite sure they could help, but somehow, they took pity on me and sent me to the intake department anyway.

I walked into the office and imagine my surprise when I saw a friendly face. It was a man I knew from the streets, from many years prior. He had gone through the program at A Safe Haven himself and was now living a stable, self-sufficient life and working there. He was living the life I dreamed of living. He understood what I needed, had mercy on me, and somehow got me into the program. How happy and grateful I was! What a stroke of divine intervention that he was there to help me and give me a chance. This was truly **God's** work and one of the many things that happened in my life that made me feel a rush of gratitude.

SAFE HAVEN SKILLS

At A Safe Haven, I had found a new, loving community with new opportunities. I came to the program ready, willing, and very open to whatever came my way.

A Safe Haven was very different than the program in Kankakee. There, the focus had been strictly on recovery, but A Safe Haven offered everything I needed to get back on my feet under one roof. They offered recovery services, but also job training, which was my main concern. I wanted to work.

A Safe Haven prepared me with the job skills I needed. They taught me how to prepare a resume and interview for a job. I also learned life skills and how to continue to stay clean from drugs. I regularly attended recovery meetings and am still in Narcotics Anonymous to this day to maintain my sobriety. Most importantly, I learned how to love myself again, and because staying sober requires relying on a higher power, I also grew closer to God.

Prayer became the best tool that I acquired at A Safe Haven. In my job and in my life, I encourage people to be grateful and PUSH— pray until something happens. I also preach hope. When you are in the midst of a struggle, it's important to hold on to HOPE—hold on, pain ends. And this too shall pass. This is an especially important lesson for someone in recovery to learn.

I learned to let people help me. There are a lot of loving people at A Safe Haven that will help you if you want to accept their help.

That means following the program guidelines and actively participating in your journey to self-sufficiency. They're there to help...but I learned that I had to do the work myself.

In the year that I lived at A Safe Haven, I learned so many things I needed to learn to live a productive life. They all made a positive impact on my ability to thrive. I now faithfully attend the Apostolic Church of **God** and I am on the security ministries there. I also attend self-help meetings regularly, which forces you to stay connected, and stay on your desired life path.

THRIVING DAILY

All of the help I've received from A Safe Haven and my church has cultivated an ever-present "attitude of gratitude" with me wherever I go. I thank **God** regularly for the little things that most people take for granted, like the birds, the bees, the flowers, and the trees. Where once I was lost, I am now found. I love my life today!

I live by the two great commandments: Love the Lord with all your heart and soul and love your neighbor as yourself. I have learned that if you give love, you will receive love. I feel like someone who plants seeds every day as I make myself available to speak with those who are struggling. I plant seeds of hope and love, then stand back and watch them grow. That's what A Safe Haven is all about.

I have been in recovery for nine years now, and my family is reunited. I haven't been given a second chance at life—it was actually a seventh chance after being shot six times. I have married the mother of two of my children and we have been married for six years. **God** is good. I'm also grateful for the workforce development program at A Safe Haven that helped trained me for the work I do today. I am employed at A Safe Haven and I work in front desk security, in reception, and also as a bus driver for the organization. I drive people from A Safe Haven to wherever they need to go. It's an especially happy day when I can move someone out of the shelter and into an apartment of their own, just as someone did for me several years ago. I enjoy working and giving back to the people who did so much for me, and I enjoy motivating and sharing my love and inspiration with others in the program.

I named this story Mr. Grateful because that's what best describes me. I'm grateful for my wife, my family, and I'm grateful for all that **God** has done for me. I am grateful for A Safe Haven, and especially Neli and Brian Rowland, and Mark Mulroe. They are true angels.

A Safe Haven literally saved my life, and I am grateful that I found **God** and that He is still molding me. I'm also grateful for life today and to be able to live one day at a time in recovery. With continued hard work and the support of A Safe Haven, I have achieved a life I had only dreamt about. And for that, I will always be Mr. Grateful.

FINAL THOUGHTS

I think that there needs to be more facilities like A Safe Haven to help and support the homeless population. We need more low-income housing and I believe that homelessness should be at the forefront of issues to be solved. We need leaders in federal government, like the president, and those in state government like the governors, and the city-level officials like the mayors and aldermen to unite and bring this issue to the forefront because it truly needs to be addressed.

Everyone can help the issue of homelessness by donating their time and resources to places like A Safe Haven that make such a difference for the homeless. Another way to help is to get the word out about the program. I carry business-sized cards to pass out to people I meet who are in need of the services provided at A Safe Haven. The cards communicate what services are available at A Safe Haven and an invitation to come to the shelter. If you refer someone to A Safe Haven and also give them the bus fare to get there, you've shown someone love!

After living 35 years as a heroin addict and being shot six times, Wilbert Lee is very grateful to be sober and employed at A Safe Haven as front desk security, receptionist, and driver.

ALEJANDRA CANO

"Having become so adept at existing, I forgot how to live."

Graduating Class: 2014
Length of Stay: 5 months
Current Status: Entrepreneur

MY JOURNEY OF INFLUENCE AND DISCOVERY

I was born in Santiago, Chile to parents who took up the cause for the country's democracy when the military, in conjunction with the U.S. government at the time, funded and engaged in a coup to seize control of its resources. My parents took a stand against the perpetrators of the heinous atrocities committed against the citizens of Chile. This act would affect our family for my entire life.

My parents were incarcerated, systematically tortured, and held in a concentration camp. Eventually, a human rights organization intervened and helped us procure safe passage to the U.S. when I was one and a half years old. It would be over a decade before I returned to Chile. Soon after our family's arrival in the U.S., my parents divorced, and my mother left to pursue a life in social work in Nicaragua. I remained with my father in Chicago.

TEEN TRAUMA

When I was thirteen, I returned to Chile to be with my mother as part of a "returned citizens" program aimed at those who were exiled during the Pinochet regime. Unfortunately, some time after we arrived, she was detained by the CNI (National Information Center Agency) and disappeared for days. Nobody knew where she was. We began to believe she was killed. Turns out, she was tortured and fled Chile again. I remained in the country with my twenty-year-old sister.

For most teens, fourteen is an age of influence and discovery and it was no different for me. I found love and embarked on an exploration that culminated in pregnancy. I was paralyzed by fear and worry and wondered, *how long can I hide this?* The answer was five months, when I could no longer hide the baby bump and word of my pregnancy reached my mother who flew to Chile immediately. I was subjected to an intensely traumatizing abortion that left me with feelings of abandonment and loneliness. I was sedated, having the life inside of me ripped away against my will.

My search for anything to fill the void of lost innocence eventually led me to my home's liquor cabinet. The "friend" I grew dependent upon sat on the highest shelf of the corner cabinet, between the dish towels and extra hand soap.

During this time, I was unable to establish roots or really get a sense of my true identity as I shuttled between Chile, Nicaragua, and Chicago. The instability left me feeling isolated and caused me to sink further into substance abuse and self-harming behaviors that would eventually escalate into full blown addiction.

I was training to become a dancer when cocaine and amphetamines came into the picture. Despite my small frame, my dance instructor incessantly pressured me to lose weight. I began to realize the drugs helped me accomplish this goal and offered a bonus feeling of numbness and euphoria that helped me escape pain. Regular use became normal. At home, in school, and socially, I had unknowingly developed a warped sense of bliss at an age when every aspect of my character and body was still in development.

FREEDOM AND SLAVERY

In 1996, and as an adult, I prematurely decided to move to Chicago by myself, determined to make my own path. Whether I was building a future or following easier access to drugs is a debate that still rages in my head, even today. Freedom, however, is fickle and requires extraordinary effort and discipline. My substance abuse issues were lurking in the shadows.

At first, I began supporting myself by working in the service industry. My substance abuse increased and my addiction was like a reaper being fed souls. It had an insatiable hunger, and so began my decades long dance with the demons that would ravish my health, sanity, and eventually bring me to my knees on the doorstep of A Safe Haven.

I could never outrun the feeling of being chased by a rabid dog who was frothing at the mouth, ready to pounce. The repercussions were becoming painfully obvious. I was no longer able to sustain gainful employment, wasn't studying or learning anything healthy, and was running in place, sweating from the effort of having to stand still. I was learning all the wrong lessons from the wrong people.

After a few years, I became pregnant once again and was painfully torn between the normal fears of expectant mothers and the feeling of betraying the life I was denied eight years earlier. *How dare I bring this life into the world after the terrible fate of my own?* I thought. The funny thing about shadows is that they are seen when light is blocked, but they are always there, creeping slowly around my body, never to be outrun. Only at night do they leave me in peace. That's when the loneliness sets in.

I promised myself that I would not subject my unborn child to the abandonment I felt as a youth. Nine months of sobriety allowed me to think clearly and develop hopes and dreams. The birth of my son was exhilarating, a moment that splits a life into a clear before and after.

Within days though, my "old friend" alcohol came to visit, and I welcomed it with open arms. My other "old friends" didn't miss a beat in joining me as well, leaving me in the wake of tired days and wasted nights. Broken promises became my reality. I numbed the pain once again and drew upon my old paradigms...influence and discovery.

A few years after my son's arrival, I was introduced to heroin. We became "best friends." The unrelenting hunger that gripped my soul was now satiated and while I held onto anything, heroin would not release me. I was sitting at a gambling table playing Texas hold'em, facing a professional player dressed like a lounge singer as a distraction from my quickly depleting bank account. This eventually led to a string of arrests for theft, possession, and driving under the influence. My illusion of control kept me fighting a war that I had lost long ago. This is when my second child was born.

We lived with my mother who provided food and shelter until I lost my first child in a bitter custody battle. Soon after, my mom decided to leave Chicago. More trouble ensued. My loss checklist reached a low I could have never imagined. No friends and family? Check. No employment, food and shelter? Check. No hope and self-respect? Check. My second son and my life were all that remained.

My descent into homelessness came quickly and lasted many years. I bounced between sleeping on the street and shelters within a harsh cycle of daily chasing and procuring. The demon did anything to keep the chase alive and taught me to survive in a brutal reality filled with shrewd eyes, cold hearts, imitation friendships, corrupt law enforcement practices, and various other predatory scenarios. I was repeatedly arrested for theft, but the last time was different. I was mandated to house arrest although I was homeless. Irony can be cruel.

I was referred to A Safe Haven where my redemption began. Not knowing how to respond or what to expect, they took me in and gave me a sense of belonging and humility. I no longer had the delusion of eminence, the fantasy of being part of the shoot-up, all-star team. I learned what hitting rock bottom meant and realized mine had already passed. I had a new trajectory, born in a promise made in a somber courtroom hallway that I was determined to keep. I was flooded with the warm rains of hope.

NEW CHALLENGES

After a month of my body attacking me with the ferocity of a prize fighter, I labored toward the dreadful cure. The mind fog lifted, and the lighthouse was in sight, shining like a beautiful Chicago skyscraper on a sun-drenched August morning. It had been years since I could string together coherent thoughts; the liberation took my breath away. The shackles were falling off and I finally held the key to the entire journey into Hell's lair. Having become so adept at existing, I forgot how to live. Did I ever fully grasp how to live? I'm not entirely sure...

A Safe Haven taught me to appreciate things in my life I had taken for granted and gave me a sense of autonomy and responsibility. I felt appreciated, valued, and independent, a part of this world and its story. The world is in me and part of my story too.

I currently have more than six years in recovery. This meandering road has led me to personal happiness and professional independence. I have found the thing I always yearned for...complete freedom. I am currently the owner of my own cleaning business in Chicago, aptly named Namaste Solutions. I live with my youngest son, now fifteen years old, who is on the gold honor roll. My oldest son has found his own path and is successful in his own right.

In life, success and accountability work together. After nearly twenty years, I visited my father and extended family in Chile. Upon my return, I was detained for secondary inspection by Immigration &

Customs Enforcement (ICE) while they reviewed my background. My passport and my lawful permanent residency card were held, and I had to undergo a secondary inspection due to irregularities that triggered immigration concerns. The officer allowed me to return home and so began a completely different struggle that has been exceeding difficult.

I am now currently in the deportation defense process supported by a legal team from a well-known agency familiar with refugee stories. They are helping me defend myself against my removal from the U.S., the place where I grew up and the only place I call home. The law views me as a moral failure and is proceeding with a process that criminalizes people who suffer with addiction and the poor choices made because of it.

The irony of not becoming a citizen in the past is not lost on me. I entered this country legally, as a refugee toddler. I qualified for citizenship but was not included in the process with my parents as a minor and did not wish to seek it while I was consumed by addiction. Now, I might lose everything. My sons, who are both U.S. citizens, would not return with me if I am deported to Chile and permanently barred from entering the U.S. ever again. It is a thought that torments me daily and has been made more severe by the pandemic.

This is where my story is now as I continue my journey of influence and discovery. I am thankful to have weathered the torrential storm of addiction, mental illness, and spiritual bankruptcy. I love who I have become and am grateful to those who have reached out to lend me a helping hand along the way. I'm hopeful that in the future, I will be able to look back and see this as a time of redemption.

FINAL THOUGHTS

I will be elated when substance abuse is treated as the illness it really is rather than being perceived and treated as a self-created, moral failure.

With love and empathy, we can heal. By showing compassion to those who we believe may not deserve it, our collective character will leap up toward light and love. By helping people find and secure safe spaces where they have a real opportunity to heal, redeem themselves of their mistakes and become healthy contributors of our society, we will all have the soulful connections we so passionately desire and deserve. We may all exist as beings of beautiful influence...and discovery.

After escaping political oppression in Chile as a toddler and surviving years of substance abuse and homelessness, Alejandra is the mother of two sons, currently resides in Chicago and is the owner of Namaste Solutions.

BELINDA MCKINLEY

"This was the model that worked."

Graduating Class: 2006
Length of Stay: 9 months
Current Status: Program Manager at ASHF

NEW BEGINNINGS

I decided to share my story with the hope that someone would be inspired to recognize a very special model of programming that led me out of despair and homelessness and into self-sufficiency and independence. I know that many people have had the same flight, the same fight, the same crisis and hopelessness.

My story began when I was a teenager. I was never abused or neglected as a child; my mom did the best that she could as a single parent, but we grew up in poverty. After my father died when I was two, my mom had to raise twelve kids on her own. I was in high school when my life took a bad turn. I did okay academically. I took business classes, learned how to type, and had dreams of becoming a paralegal. This was before the computer era, and if you could type, that meant you had "clerical skills." But due to negative social influences and economic factors, I started drinking and smoking marijuana.

LIVING IN VIOLENCE

After high school, I was able to obtain some clerical positions but could not hold a steady job. After-work parties and drinks at lunchtime prevented that. My alcoholism was progressing, and I didn't know it at the time. I could not see the grips of addiction coming my way. I had become an alcoholic that had not yet hit rock bottom. Then I met a man...

In the beginning, our relationship was great. He treated me like a lady. He respected me, bragged about me, and I became family. But that all changed after I moved in with him. Alcohol would turn him into a monster. The more he drank, the worse the beatings got. And he would drink every day. I lived with domestic violence for fourteen years. I slept with it every night. I had no place to go. My self-confidence was in the toilet. I did not think I could make it without him. Or at least he beat that thought into me. Every time I would leave, he would somehow find me. He even broke my arm and cracked my ribs.

I tried to hide the black eyes with makeup and large sunglasses. He would humiliate me in front of my friends. If I did not hustle and somehow come up with the money for our addiction, all day, every day, he would beat me. I was stripped of every ounce of self-respect and dignity that I ever had. Violence had become a normal part of my daily life. I felt so worthless and so hopeless, but again, I had nowhere to go. At that time, there were no laws against domestic violence like there are now. I would call the police and they would just have him sleep it off in the bullpen and let him go. There was no arrest, no charges, no court dates.

In addition to the domestic violence, I also struggled with alcohol and substance use. I used drugs and alcohol to mask and cover my feelings of hopelessness, despair, and self-hatred. I hated my life, the way that I was living, the things that I was doing, and who I had become. I was homeless, unemployable, and struggling with addiction. I had degraded myself. My family wanted nothing to do with me and had taken my children from me. I was in no shape or position to be a mother.

I was stealing to fuel my addictions, and after my first arrest, I was facing a felony offense. I went through a series of arrests and time in the state prison system before I had a life- changing experience during my last arrest.

While locked up, I became so sick from the withdrawals that I began vomiting. I was too weak to stand up and lay on the floor in my own vomit. I had finally hit rock bottom. The more I cried out, the more I was ignored. The officers were not willing to help; they must have seen it all the time. I thought I was going to die. I was so sick, and so humiliated, I knew I just couldn't keep living that way.

I had a deep desire to get my life together, but I didn't know where to start. I was homeless and all of my friends were in the same position. My family had lost all hope in me. I had no stability, nowhere to go, and I just wanted change.

FROM ROCK BOTTOM TO ROLE MODEL

When you're on parole and do not have stable housing, the Illinois Department of Corrections works with recovery homes and other agencies to provide housing for you. IDOC will pay for approximately 60 days of housing. After that, you're on your own. Since I was homeless, I was offered a bed at A Safe Haven. I knew that I was not willing to go back to the beatings and my mom was not willing to house me, so I decided to go. I thought it would just be another institution. I had been to so many—program after program, hospital after hospital, in and out of jails and shelters. I was so tired of that life.

I arrived at A Safe Haven in August of 2005 and I didn't know what to expect. At first, I was impressed because it didn't look like an institution. It was a courtyard building that looked like apartments. I went to the office, completed the admission process, and was escorted to an apartment that I would share with another recovering alcoholic. I was given the rules and policies, and I adapted immediately.

We were housed in an apartment with a full kitchen, living room, dining room, and bedrooms. This was the first time in my 20-year history of homelessness and addiction that I saw a model like this. It was unique. What I didn't know was that this model was designed to teach us sober living skills.

We started with the basics: how to buy food and clean and keep up an apartment, how to be responsible, go shopping, obtain credentials, and return on time. They're basic life skills that someone like me, an alcoholic, did not possess. I had become so unstable that I had to start from the beginning.

The program structure was so important. We had to attend mandatory functions for education on recovery from drugs and alcohol. I began to look forward to the groups. I never knew how much structure and discipline would play a major role in getting my life together. My life slowly improved. For the first time, I felt comfortable and I knew that I was not leaving this place. They would not be able to get rid of me.

I stayed at A Safe Haven for nine months and during that time, I had the opportunity to work with a very special man, the program director "Skip" Land. Skip was very instrumental in creating and developing the state laws that govern recovery homes. Not only did he teach me the model of recovery, but he was very influential in my own personal recovery. He taught me how to remain sober and how to teach others. I attended professional development trainings and learned how to manage recovery homes. I became a peer leader and monitor. The people at A Safe Haven saw something in me that I didn't see in myself and they gave me an opportunity to turn my life around. I was about to begin a new journey in my life.

I also felt safe. Being housed at A Safe Haven Damen site in Rodgers Park was the catalyst for leaving my abusive significant other. The facility was far away from the west side, so he had no idea where to locate me and I didn't share with him or any of our friends where I was. I was determined to change my life and remained in Rodgers Park for almost a year.

After consistently attending professional development trainings, I was able to obtain a license with the state as an NCRS, a National Certified Recovery Specialist. In addition, I obtained a Certified Alcohol and Drug Counselor (CDAC) license with the State Board. I worked with the founders of A Safe Haven Foundation, Brian and Neli Rowland, and they welcomed me to the team and treated me like family.

A MODEL THAT WORKS

Brian and Neli get to know the employees who work for them. They give us personal attention and treat us like family. A Safe Haven helped me reunite with my children too and I have slowly developed a relationship with them after being absent from their lives for more than fifteen years. Through the years, Neli and Brian knew my struggles of getting my kids through college and knew that we needed an apartment. Today, I am so proud of my four adult children. Three of them have graduated college and two of them have master's degrees.

Neli and Brian were there for funerals, weddings, and graduations. We attended banquets and parades together. I never saw an agency that was so invested in their team. I belonged to a new family; a family that had a mission to save lives.

A Safe Haven gave me an opportunity to work with others who had dealt with some of the same struggles that I had experienced. I began working for A Safe Haven as a case aide before being promoted to case manager, then to supervisor, and finally to my current role, as program manager for the criminal justice division at A Safe Haven

Foundation. In addition, I am currently attending Northeastern Illinois University and anticipate graduating in December of 2020 with a degree in human services with a minor in criminal justice. As of June 2020, I celebrated fourteen years as an employee at A Safe Haven Foundation. My history at A Safe Haven has provided experiential knowledge in my fields of study, and I currently am a program manager who oversees the day-to-day operations for A Safe Havens' Criminal Justice Division, a position I have held for the past four years.

A Safe Haven helped save my life. I went from a life of hopelessness and despair to a life of stability and helping others, all because of the A Safe Haven model. It provided stable housing, addressed the substance use and the domestic violence, identified my skill level, and provided training and the foundation I needed to be successful. This model reached the root cause of what kept me hopeless, helpless, and homeless. I have participated in so many programs, institutions, treatment centers, hospitals, and none were able to pull me out of the pits of despair. This was the model that worked.

I will be celebrating 16 years of sobriety in a couple of months, and I remain passionate about helping others who are suffering from homelessness, addiction, domestic violence, etc. I believe in paying it forward, so I'm glad I can pass on a gift that was so freely given to me.

I have so much passion for the work that we do at A Safe Haven Foundation and am so proud to be a part of an organization that helps people who are in crisis. Whatever it may be—mental health, substance use, homelessness, unemployment, literacy skills—A Safe Haven can and will turn it around. We are on the front line constantly fighting to help people in crisis. I have seen countless lives repaired, revitalized, restored, and improved, all because of a very special model and a very special organization that is committed and dedicated to helping people. Thank you, Brian and Neli Rowland, for A Safe Haven. Thank you for the cause and for the mission. And thank you for helping me turn my life around.

FINAL THOUGHTS

Every day at A Safe Haven I get a visual of the homeless population and their needs. Homelessness is at a critical point in our country right now. So many people are not only without housing but without education, job skills, and even nutritional food because of socioeconomic disparities.

We need more than just shelters. We need programming. We need to provide the services people need to become self-sufficient, like education, job readiness, physical and mental health, financial literacy, and more. When I came to A Safe Haven, it was programs like these that made me able to work my way back into independent living. It wasn't just giving me a bed or a warm meal. It was giving me so much more. We're so concerned with getting the homeless off the streets or off the train, but we should be more concerned with raising them to the highest level of their individual success, whatever that may be for them. And that requires programming.

How do we call attention to the need for more programming? Writing local leaders and Congress to request more funding doesn't always meet with success. I think networking and collaboration could move the agenda forward if more private industries would partner with public resources to help those in need. However, the first step is for more of us to acknowledge just how serious the issue of homelessness is. We all need to step up to make a change!

After fleeing a domestic violence situation and struggling with alcoholism, Belinda McKinley now has four grown children, is graduating from college, and has been gainfully employed at A Safe Haven for fourteen years.

ANGALIA BIANCA

"If I didn't get help, I was going to die alone in an alley from a drug overdose or a bullet."

Graduating Class: 2012
Length of Stay: 8 months
Current Status: Anti-Violence Activist and Public Speaker

YEARS LOST, LIFE FOUND

People who meet me today would never guess that I was a heroin addict, gang member, and career criminal for thirty-six years. I first got high at the age of nine on morphine pills that my friend and I stole from his dying father's medicine cabinet. I moved on to weed, alcohol, barbiturates, and Quaaludes. I was always so high that I barely lived within reality. I liked the feeling of being completely sedated.

My family loved me so much. My grandmother, who raised me, did not drink alcohol, smoke cigarettes, or do drugs. Yet I was always out, ditching school so I could go hang out in the park to smoke weed, pop pills, and party. My family hoped I would grow out of it, but of course I never did. In the blink of an eye, thirty years were gone.

THE ADDICT'S LIFE

When I was seventeen years old, I tried heroin, and from that point on, I was addicted. Within a couple months I was so strung out that I started prostituting to pay for it. I would try to stop and go through withdrawal, but after a couple weeks or a month, I'd go right back to using.

Heroin was stronger than me and brought me to my knees, even though I thought I could deal with anything. But when I found out I was pregnant at the age of nineteen, I somehow found the strength to stay sober during my pregnancy. I was married to the baby's father and living in the Arizona desert in a trailer. He was not a heroin addict, although he drank a lot of alcohol, popped a lot of pills, and smoked a lot of marijuana.

My baby was born healthy and drug-free. But by the time he was about six weeks old, heroin was calling my name again. I followed that deafening whisper right back to a dope house with my baby in my arms to buy what I needed. I put my sleeping baby on the couch and proceeded to shoot up heroin, but because I had been clean for some time, it was too strong, and I overdosed. When I woke, I was soaking wet because my friend was throwing water and ice cubes on me to revive me. She saved my life while my beautiful little baby boy slept through the whole thing.

I tried to maintain my relationships with my family, but they all knew what was happening. They felt helpless and really didn't know what to do. Out of love, they continued to give me money, bond me out of jail, hire lawyers for me and completely enable me. I continued to run around, commit crimes to support my habit, get high, and party, always leaving my children with my grandma.

After ten years of addiction, my father finally demanded that I go into a twenty-eight-day detox. I complied, not because I wanted to stop getting high but to stay in good standing with my family. I got high the whole time I was there, thanks to my drug dealer who visited me and brought heroin. I found myself in the bathroom of my hospital room, shooting up heroin every day. On other occasions, I went to short-term detox programs. They would let me stay a few days and then release me with no resources or clear path of what to do next. So, I would go back to the only thing I knew—the streets and heroin.

Eventually, my family disowned me, leaving me to fend for myself. I lost myself on the west side of Chicago and never returned home. Deep down inside, I knew it would hurt them if they ever saw me and as much as it hurt me, I wouldn't go back.

I was thankful for my family because every time I'd have a baby and could not take care of it, they would help. I ended up having five children while I was strung out and living on the streets. It turned into a life-long lifestyle and I never in a million years thought I could do anything to change it. I figured these were the cards I was dealt, and I had to survive.

After I had my fifth child in 1997, things were so bad that I was homeless and walking around Chicago with a newborn baby girl. I slept wherever I could and somehow managed to have formula and diapers for her in addition to supporting my expensive heroin habit. I had to hustle every single day and my baby came along. After a few months, I knew there was no way I could keep her. I called my mother, and she took custody of my daughter. I always had a sick feeling in my stomach when I'd have to give up one of my children. I could have been a good mother, but with substance abuse in my life, motherhood was never going to work out for me.

CRIMINAL MATTERS

Alone on the streets, addicted and homeless, I would wake up thinking, *God, do we really have to do this all over again?* I honestly didn't care if I lived or died. I was constantly in and out of the Cook County jail and I ended up doing a total of twelve years in the state penitentiary in Illinois with seven different sentences. So many times, I stood in front of a Cook County judge who sent me to the penitentiary, and every time I got out, I went right back to the only life I knew.

I was in prison when my grandmother died in 2004. She had raised me from a baby, and I loved her more than anyone in the world. She died with a broken heart. Her last words on her deathbed were to her son, my Uncle Joey. In her very weak voice she told him, "Joey, please take care of my Angela." Then she died. My name was the last word she spoke, and I have to live with that.

In 2010, I received my seventh prison sentence. The Cook County judge told me he was going to recommend I go to A Safe Haven upon my release. It wasn't mandatory; it was totally up to me so while I was doing my time, I didn't pay much attention to the option.

On January 11, 2011, my father died while I was in prison. Somehow my father's death gave me life! I began to realize that if I didn't get help, I was going to die alone in an alley from a drug overdose or a bullet. For the first time, I really wanted to change but had no idea how.

I was finally paroled from the Illinois Department of Corrections, Lincoln prison on August 9, 2011, and went to a friend's house. After being there two days, I realized it was a mistake. There were drugs in the house, and I knew that if I stayed there, I would end up addicted, back on the streets, and ultimately back in prison or dead. I remembered that Judge Porter had given me the option of A Safe Haven, so I begged my parole officer to transfer me there. She told me I'd be okay and I should stay where I was, but I knew I would be doomed if I stayed, so I called A Safe Haven myself.

I was literally crying on the phone and begging them to please let me come. The program manager on the other end asked me if I had money to get on the train and told me to come to their facility on the north side of Chicago and that she would call the parole officer and make arrangements for me to stay there. When I arrived, I was so happy because I knew this was my only chance. Everyone was so kind to me. I was hungry, and they fed me. I had a soft warm bed to sleep in, and I was truly grateful.

THE SAFE HAVEN EFFECT

In the beginning, living at A Safe Haven was a struggle. I wasn't used to rules. I was told to wash the office window with Windex every night at 8 p.m. Many nights I would be watching TV and I'd forget about the 8 p.m. chore. The counselor would find me and say, "Aren't you supposed to be doing something right now?"

"Oh yeah, the window, I'm sure it's clean. it didn't rain or anything!" I'd reply.

Then the counselor would say to me in a very loving voice, "Bianca, either you participate, or you'll have to leave the program."

Of course, I immediately thought about an abandoned building with roaches and rats and I'd say," Where's the Windex and the paper towels?"

Looking back, I now understand they were teaching me accountability and responsibility. I had to be somewhere at the same time, every day, to do one small thing. Before I knew it, two months went by, then three, and I was still sober, I started volunteering and offering to do more.

Eventually they transferred me to the main facility at 2750 West Roosevelt Road. I was concerned about living on the corner of California and Roosevelt, where I used to buy heroin, but my counselor gave me the best advice. She said, "Bianca, stay focused and just get on the bus and go to your destination." I took her advice to heart and would hear her words every time I set foot out the door.

A Safe Haven helped me get my first Illinois state ID card in twenty-nine years. I was so excited that I must have showed it to every passenger on that bus back to A Safe Haven. I began looking for a job, which is not very easy as a convicted felon. I was hired part time at a fast-food place downtown. It was my first job in more than twenty-five years.

One morning, a counselor asked if I'd be willing to volunteer to answer the phones at the front desk. She said I was polite and had a good rapport with people. I loved doing that job and felt very important. I started noticing people looking at me with respect, and I really liked that feeling. I never wanted to lose respect again!

Every time I'd get my paycheck, I would deposit it all into my newly opened savings account at Bank of America so I could someday get a studio apartment. Through hard work and the guidance of the staff at A Safe Haven, I moved to a better paying, full-time job.

I took a chance and called my mother. I could tell in her voice that I had given her hope after I told her where I was and how long I had been there.

I lived at A Safe Haven more than eight months. When I left in March of 2012, I had my own apartment, a decent living wage job, and my family was beginning to believe in me again. I have become a law-abiding, tax-paying, sober citizen.

Now, I work relentlessly to help people in the populations I once inhabited. I have been blessed to travel around the world giving speeches and trainings on violence prevention, social change, and homelessness.

I would not be where I am today without A Safe Haven and Neli Vazquez Rowland. They are my family, and I stay connected with them and volunteer there regularly. I give all Glory to God, for it was He who put A Safe Haven in my path. For that, I am eternally grateful and humbled.

FINAL THOUGHTS

Looking back, I realize how hard it was to live a lifestyle where I woke up daily in full heroin withdrawal and I was always in survival mode and in and out of jail and prison. Today, I work long hours in social services. I give back to help homelessness, addiction, violence prevention, and more.

Not only did A Safe Haven give me the tools to get sober, but also to stay sober, to succeed in life, and become self-sufficient. Today I work relentlessly to change policy. I feel the solution to homelessness is at our fingertips and that is to fund and implement more programs with a holistic approach, coupled with wraparound services like they offer at A Safe Haven. I believe there should be A Safe Haven location in every city across the country because it really works. They have thousands of real stories of success from real people. I know because I am one of them!

Also, anyone who wants to contribute to the solution can just volunteer their help, because a homeless person is invisible to mainstream society. Just acknowledging them makes them feel like a worthy human being. Handing them a meal or a coat will make the world of difference to them. Also, people should call their legislators regularly because we must change how society has marginalized far too many undeserved communities and populations.

As I always say...

"There's nothing stronger than the woman who rose from the cold floor she was left to die on to make a productive life for herself."

After battling substance abuse and homelessness for thirty-six years, Angalia Bianca found a new life at A Safe Haven. She now has a bachelor's degree in inner city studies and works for a major university as a data and evaluation specialist and an expert in the field of violence prevention, homelessness, and addiction.

KAREN LEATO

"Living at A Safe Haven has truly turned our lives around and helped to make us the strong family that we are today."

Graduating Class: 2013
Length of Stay: 7 months
Current Status: Librarian at a School

EARNING THE KEYCHAIN

My name is Karen Leato and I have seven children—four girls and three boys. The oldest child is by one man, and the other six are by my husband. My married life was tumultuous, filled with emotional and physical abuse. This came to an end on November 4, 2011 when my husband officially left us and never returned.

HEARTBREAK OF HOMELESSNESS

For a year I struggled to pay the rent and support my children as a single mother, but we just couldn't keep up. We officially became homeless on June 1, 2012 when we were officially evicted from our apartment in Cicero, Illinois with no place to go.

The eviction split up the family. My oldest daughter, who was twenty, got married to a wonderful man. Our youth pastor's family in Berwyn took in my oldest son, who was thirteen at the time, and my twelve-year-old daughter was able to live with the parents of a leader in an organization in Cicero that we had been involved with for many years. It served underprivileged children with educational and spiritual programs and resources.

In desperation to find shelter for me, my eight and nine-year-olds, and my twin six-year-olds, we found a shelter who would take us for the night at the City of Chicago Homeless Referral Center located at 10 S. Kedzie. We stayed there for the first three nights that we were homeless. To get into the shelter, you had to check-in at eight o'clock to claim beds. Everyone slept in the same room, on a cot, with the lights on all night. It was better than sleeping on the street, but I was very concerned for my children and I was so grateful when on the fourth night, at around ten o'clock, they loaded our family into a van and took us to A Safe Haven. Someone had taken pity on us and arranged our transfer to A Safe Haven, since places to house mothers and children were scarce in the city.

NEW LIFE

The conditions at A Safe Haven were like a dream come true! My children and I could all stay in the same private room and we could sleep with the lights off at night. And the only people we had to share a bathroom with were the people in the room next door.

Everyone was able to get what they needed at A Safe Haven. We always ate well at the wonderful cafeteria that served us delicious breakfast, lunch, and dinner. There was also a terrific Thanksgiving dinner, a Fourth of July BBQ, an Easter egg hunt, a Halloween party, and an amazing, stupendous Christmas event. Every year they hold an awesome 5K Run to End Homelessness, which is inspiring and brings hope to the hopeless. It also gave us all some great exercise and enabled the community to understand what A Safe Haven does and why they need their donations.

While my children were in school, I attended classes to learn computer skills and how to write a resume. I met a mixture of single moms, veterans, and people who were under house arrest, wearing electronic monitoring ankle bracelets, and being held there instead of sitting in jail while they awaited their court dates. We got along with everyone. When I arrived at A Safe Haven, I had thirteen years of abstinence from alcohol under my belt. The stress of being homeless, a single parent, separated from my children and living with uncertainty about the future would have been enough to send me back to drinking. However, because I was at A Safe Haven, I was able to attend AA recovery groups and with their support, I was able to manage my many life stresses without succumbing to the bottle.

We learned so much from so many different people, and the experience humbled me as well. Many of the people living at a Safe Haven had made grave mistakes because of substance abuse, but A Safe Haven was a great place to build a second chance. I was grateful to be in an environment that understood what it was like to have those challenges.

My kids were happy at A Safe Haven too. We were all taught structure and discipline everyday with our schedules and chores. We still all use the same skills today! My kids were picked up every morning for school by a special bus and dropped back off safely in time for dinner.

The shelter was very family friendly, and seemingly made for moms with kids. There were family movie nights and game nights, and the children were able to play and spend time together. My children made many friends while living at A Safe Haven. The playground on the lawn in the back of the facility was a wonderful place to get some fresh air and exercise. There were beautiful flowers planted everywhere to brighten things up thanks to A Safe Haven's landscaping business, which provides work for many people and beautifies many places in Chicago. I made close friends with the moms at a Safe Haven who had experiences similar to mine. I still keep in contact with many of them.

My classes and my teachers all inspired me. They were honest and realistic about everything they taught us and encouraging about our future options. The staff built us up and gave us a sense of purpose and our dignity. We all felt safe inside the building and enjoyed the many programs that were offered. My caseworker helped me find services I needed and looked for an apartment for us that I could afford once I got a job. In one of the inspirational speeches given by Neli Vazquez Rowland, the founder of A Safe Haven, she said that we should strive for the day that we get a key to our own apartment. On that day we would be given an A Safe Haven key chain so every time we unlocked our front door, we would remember how far we have come. I kept that keychain in mind and reached for it, the entire seven months I stayed at A Safe Haven.

I was so happy when my case manager gave us the news that we could move into one of the 3-bedroom apartments managed by A Safe Haven in North Lawndale. It was a happy day the first time I turned my new apartment key with my A Safe Haven keychain, just as Neli had promised. I cried tears of joy and relief.

BACK ON TRACK

Within a month, all my children were back living under my roof. We were so excited to together again! We lived in the A Safe Haven apartment for two years. It was a wonderful experience and we felt safe and protected. Eventually, though, we saved our money and moved back to Cicero where we originally came from. I was able to get my old job back, working on the lunch staff with the Cicero schools. I felt like I had come full circle back to a stable life in our hometown.

Living at A Safe Haven has truly turned our lives around and helped to make us the strong family that we are today. I am extremely thankful for what they were able to do for us, and I can't imagine where we would have been if we didn't have this opportunity.

Eight years after being homeless and twenty-two years in sobriety, I still use my A Safe Haven keychain to open our front door. There is so much more I could say about A Safe Haven and why there should be more organizations like theirs in the world, but to sum it up, we are forever grateful for A Safe Haven and our time spent there. Every time I open my front door, I see my keychain and remember how far I've come. Full circle!

FINAL THOUGHTS

Few people, and especially politicians, rarely understand how quickly ordinary people are becoming homeless. So many of us work tirelessly to support our families as best we can, but our income doesn't cover the bills we have to pay. I have seen many hardworking people trying to move themselves and their families out of dangerous neighborhoods and better themselves with jobs and education. However, tey are still stuck and need support to move forward.

It took me three years to get back to Cicero because of economic reasons. The only place I could afford to live with all of my children was Lawndale or Englewood. It's discouraging that there isn't more affordable housing available in safer areas.

Another issue plaguing so many homeless families is mental and behavioral health. These are real concerns that unfortunately, have limited resources available for helping other people, and the facilities that do exist have a very long waiting list. A Safe Haven offers an elegant solution to both challenges of affordable living and treatment for mental health issues and they do it all under one roof. There should be more locations of A Safe Haven around the country!

Single mother Karen Leato experienced years of homelessness as a victim of domestic violence, but after a stay with A Safe Haven, she now works today for the Cicero School District, supporting herself and her family.

MARSHALL GALBREATH

"If you trust the process, you can have a very good life."

Graduating Class: 2010
Length of Stay: 4 months
Current Status: Food Service Director/Executive Chef

LIVING MY VALUES

———————

Everyone has a story, and this is mine. As I sit and reflect on my journey, I can't help but smile. I am truly proud of how far I have come because it hasn't always been easy.

I was born and raised on the South side of Chicago. Growing up, I was raised by my mother and father, who was a U.S. Army veteran. But as life takes turns, so did mine. I was later also raised by my stepmom, grandmother, and aunt. Although I grew up with different people, they all raised me with morals, values, and integrity. I am sad to say that although I was raised well, that did not stop me from making some bad choices. It was those choices that led me into the abyss.

BECOMING A "MAN"

Before going off the rails, I entered the U.S. Army where I was a satellite communication operator. I received my Honorable Discharge after service and started looking for ways to transition back into civilian life. But that transition was much harder than I expected. It was a struggle for me. I made some mistakes, and I wasn't sure what I wanted to do in life. It was a difficult time and not having a sense of purpose didn't help. That's when I began making some bad decisions.

Merriam-Webster's Dictionary defines the word "abyss" as meaning "a bottomless pit." That's exactly where I was in my mental and emotional well-being. This darkness led me to a life of addiction and drugs. I went to jail a few times and my emotional, spiritual, and physical health was a disaster. I definitely paid for my mistakes. But in the midst of that dark time in my life and having truly hit dark bottom, I had what some people would call a "spiritual awakening." Now I know there are many people who suddenly turn to God for help when they get into trouble, then go back to doing what they were doing. This is true for some, but I can honestly say that on the day of my final arrest I was overwhelmed with joy. It was a relief from the life of bondage I had been living because of my own choices.

The police looked at me like I was disturbed, because they couldn't understand why I was happy to be getting arrested. They didn't understand I was experiencing the exact moment of complete surrender, and the reckless life I had been living was now over. Of course, I knew I had to deal with the consequences of my actions, but to me that was just the first step towards a life of peace and tranquility.

During my stay in one of the State of Illinois facilities, I worked day and night on strengthening my mind and emotional stability. No walking the yard, playing cards, and getting "swole" pumping iron. No time for any of that. I was consumed with planning for a life of true peace and prosperity.

During my stay, there were a couple of tragic events that caused me despair. I was called not once, but twice to the captain's office. The first time was to let me know that my grandfather had passed, and then a couple of months later, to let me know that my father had passed. I was heartbroken and it was a time of deep reflection, sadness, and anger. Because of my bad choices, I had taken myself away from them and was not able to share in their last moments. Each had been an honorable "man" in every sense of the word and had passed on values of strength and integrity that I had long neglected to nurture in myself. After a few days of mourning, I made the decision to honor them by doing what they had wanted me to do for the longest time. I would become a man myself, and that's exactly what I did.

In prison, I joined a veteran's group which brought in outside vet administrators to assist us with discharge planning and connect us with available resources upon our release. My vet rep told me about a shelter called A Safe Haven Foundation. When he told me it was a shelter, I immediately rejected the suggestion. There was no way on Earth was I going to a shelter that would give you a sandwich, a bowl of soup, and tell you to get out. I wasn't doing that! Then he explained all that was offered at A Safe Haven and the opportunities I would have if I gave the program a chance. I reminded myself that my previous way of transitioning back into society hadn't worked. I may as well give it a shot, I thought.

LEADER AND TEACHER

I arrived at A Safe Haven homeless, tired, and on parole with an ankle bracelet. It was April 12, 2010. The place really did become a "safe haven" for me in every way. They told me if you trust and follow the process, good things will happen. That it is exactly what I did because I knew this might be my last chance to heal myself and turn my life around.

In my early days at A Safe Haven, I remember having conversations with the founders, Neli Vazquez Rowland and her husband, Brian Rowland. I always admired them because despite overseeing a large nonprofit and having many important things to do and events to attend, they always stopped in the hallways and talked to the residents. They have good hearts and fight to keep A Safe Haven thriving and helping people like me. I'm also grateful to Mark Mulroe, the VP of A Safe Haven Foundation, who has been a strong mentor and support system for me. He has challenged me daily to reach my fullest potential and become a stronger, organizational leader. His guidance has helped me approach life analytically and contributed to my personal success.

While at A Safe Haven, I also strengthened my family relations with the support of my wife, Renea, as well as others in my family. I've lived a life of peace and tranquility which I will never give up again! Renea's undying support and love has been a strong foundation for me, and I thank God daily for allowing me to share life with her. Her strength and determination to succeed inspires me every day. I couldn't do it without her!

I am extremely happy that ten years after arriving at A Safe Haven as a resident, I am still here as a staff member. Today, my official title is Executive Chef and Food Service Director of A Safe Haven. I have earned various culinary degrees and certifications, but the pieces of paper mean much less to me than the standards they represent. I am very proud of my accomplishments, but I am more gratified by helping others at the shelter. I work for others. I often say, "It's what I can do for you; it's not about me." And I really believe it!

Not only do I serve as the Executive Chef, but I am also an instructor and teach others about culinary and how they too can become chefs. I thoroughly enjoy being an instructor and contributing to my students' development. I think what I like best is helping others hone the skills they already possess. In this community, a lot of students are told from a very young age that they aren't going to amount to anything, and they are going to end up in jail or worse.

When you hear that over and over as a child, it becomes part of your psyche. I tell them it doesn't have to be that way. I believe, if you want to put in the hard work, dedication, and sacrifices, you will succeed. I love to quote Socrates and tell my students that "I know that I know nothing." If they can accept that, then they can be taught. And I love to teach. As the students progress, there are many who are brought onboard to work in our catering social enterprise, which provides catering services throughout Chicagoland. I'm privileged and honored to be able to lead this team.

LIFEGIVING OPPORTUNITY

My life really does feel like it has come full circle. By the grace of God, A Safe Haven also brought about a reunion with my little sister, Kattrina, who walked through our doors as an employee. I hadn't seen her in a while and didn't know she had applied for a job in HR. It was a moment for the angels when we saw one another. I cried like a baby, but don't tell anyone. We went to visit our father, which was a first for me since his passing. That moment was just another confirmation of the strength of our shared love for him.

I am very grateful for all the opportunities in my life and especially for the opportunity to make something out of my life. Those values I learned as a kid never completely left me; life just knocked me down a few times and made me overlook them. Today, I am happy that I can be helpful to others and live my life with my values held high. I try to look at everything with understanding care and empathy. That is who I am today. I am proud of my journey and I could not be more excited to see what's next.

FINAL THOUGHTS

Dear readers, you probably have encountered someone on the street, pleading to you with the following spoken or unspoken messages: "Can you please spare some change? I'm trying to get something to eat. Please, can you spare a little change? I know what you're thinking but I'm NOT an addict! I'm not lazy! I don't have mental issues! I'm just someone who has experienced some hardships because I was laid off months ago. I was living paycheck to paycheck, and now I'm here."

Preventing a crisis requires active managerial control, a proactive approach in identifying potential threats, and the ability to implement programs that address the causes while providing solutions. We could prevent more people from becoming homeless by finding at-risk individuals like domestic abuse victims, the incarcerated, people with substance abuse disorders, low-income individuals, and those with mental health issues. Only then can we provide services, with the help of financial investments, political and corporate leadership, humanity, and a host of integrative programs which build partnerships.

Homelessness isn't just a local issue, but a global one that affects us all. To some politicians, there isn't any value in helping the homeless since few of them vote. For those who truly care and understand the value and importance of helping others besides self, it's imperative that we, as a society, invest in funding to create programs to assist with the root causes of homelessness, increase wages, and challenge sentencing guidelines for drug-related incarceration. Even if you do not have compassion for someone's situation, just by helping someone homeless get back up on their feet, you can contribute to society, which helps us all.

After being honorably discharged from the Army, Marshall Galbreath struggled with transition into society and endured addiction and prison before finding the help he needed at A Safe Haven. Now, he has worked as the Executive Chef and Food Service Director there for ten years, where he feeds residents three hot meals daily, oversees all catering operations, and is responsible for supervising and mentoring his staff.

NIKELCIA MARCELIN

"A Safe Haven helped remove barriers that were keeping me from reaching my goals."

Graduating Class: 2016
Length of Stay: 4 months
Current Status: Mental Health Advocate & Business Owner

INVISIBLE WOUNDS ARE EQUAL TO VISIBLE WOUNDS

Having to fight battles is hard enough; not having any help to fight them is unacceptable. As a retired logistical coordinator and staff sergeant in the U.S. Army, I mostly served overseas in Afghanistan and Korea. Yet when I returned to America, I felt like I was entering a different war zone—the raging war zone of poverty in this country. And my community was losing.

My story had humble beginnings, but I wanted to change my future. I began to explore why so many people were facing poverty. I am a decorated soldier with many talents, and I was determined to change the narrative. I went to school and wrote a book called *Are Veterans Transitioning Effectively in American Society?* I became the author and the case study, all at the same time.

ON THE RUN

My story begins with the trauma and the results of experiencing an abusive, life-threatening relationship with the father of my child. It occurred during my military service. After discharge, I went to stay with my family in Florida in fear that this relationship would haunt my new beginnings. To ensure my safety and my child's and pursue a better life, I moved to a new area undisclosed from my immediate family. I enrolled in a university away from my family and friends. During this time, I sought help and support dealing with my military trauma. For a time, my child and I felt safe in our private safe haven. But as I tried to navigate the process of claiming my veteran's benefits, (a process that would take over four years after my transition from military service), I hit obstacle after obstacle because of a system that is currently not streamlined to effectively transition veterans.

During this time, I was still also dealing with emotional trauma and PTSD from my experience in war in Afghanistan, and also underlying heinous domestic violence which would unexpectedly and ferociously trigger with certain events. When I found out that my ex-husband knew we were living in Florida, I needed to go somewhere, anywhere safe to figure out what was next. I felt the need for spiritual guidance and made the decision to travel to Illinois to attend a conference and see church leaders who I felt could give me answers. I remember a time of reflection when I fell to my knees in the church and fervently prayed, *Dear Lord, all I need is a safe haven.*

As I prepared to travel back to Florida to continue the battle for me and my child, a terrible hurricane hit and I could not return home. I spent several days exhausting my resources at a hotel to find shelter while the storm passed. Once the weather report cleared us for travel, I decided to head back to Florida and address my hardships. Then, at the airport, as I tried to pay for a flight, I found out I was the victim of identity theft. I felt the world crash down on me. Right then and there, my PTSD triggered and I panicked. I prayed in the bathroom and asked God again to provide a safe haven for me and my child.

Once I realized that all my support was exhausted and no family to reach, I headed straight to the VA and asked for help. When I went through intake, I was told that there were several organizations that could provide my child and I with temporary shelter. They gave me a list and all of a sudden, my eyes fell upon the name of one of the organizations they suggested for me—A Safe Haven. My prayer was answered. I took it as a sign that I had found my transitional living until I could get back home.

TEMPORARY HOME

When I arrived at A Safe Haven, the staff was surprised at my initial intake. The program was built to take on veterans and not the family. With prayer, A Safe Haven was able to provide us with shelter under the Department of Children and Family Services (DCFS) instead of the VA. At first, I felt ashamed and rejected by the system not having the support of the VA, but after my initial stay, A Safe Haven kept me safe and did not allow me to feel ashamed of my process. They provided much needed hospitality and resources. I was so grateful to have shelter and safety in an unfamiliar city. The program provided us a comfortable place to stay together in the same room. The organization was familiar with the plight of veterans and I was able to meet many other veterans at A Safe Haven which provided networking and comradery during this transition.

A Safe Haven had everything I needed. I appreciated the in-house community resource center for veterans, so I did not have to travel back and forth to the VA daily. Their staff was able to help me connect with VA's in different systems to sort out my benefits. My child could attend school nearby, and there was excellent security at A Safe Haven, so I always felt safe. I learned about other resources available to me both through the VA and organizations like HUD, the Department of Housing and Urban Development. A Safe Haven removed all the barriers that were keeping me from reaching my goals in pursuing an effective transition from the military.

Slowly, with the help of organizations like A Safe Haven, I began to heal my invisible wounds—the internal wounds which nobody could see surfacing and presenting themselves within my mindset, as I determined my life priorities. For years I hid behind my routine and masked my pain through activity, people, places, and things such as a career, faith, roles, and more. I thought that visible wounds were more important, but after several encounters with my invisible wounds that would not be ignored, I realized that I had to address them, or I would die. It was an emergency, and I needed help. I needed to learn how to prioritize my invisible wounds over my other needs and the weight of social pressure.

Finally, I set my emotional, mental, and spiritual health above my looks and social status. The military lifestyle taught me how to prioritize stress when you are in war; my PTSD and A Safe Haven taught me to prioritize stress management in civilian life. A Safe Haven allowed me, for the first time, to deal with both the invisible and visible wounds such as hopelessness, fear, depression, homelessness, postpartum depression, and more.

At A Safe Haven, my child found friends, socializing with the other children staying there. And as my socioeconomic and psychological conditions stabilized, so did we. My child started to excel in school and today is still performing at the highest levels of reading and math in grade level.

With A Safe Haven providing the correct resources to help me, my mind cleared and I realized I had to help others, just as I had received assistance and guidance.

I volunteered time at A Safe Haven to contribute to organizations like Social Change, where we support the needs of the community through advocacy and legislation, and helping with local campaigns, including the alderman election in the 20th district. Giving back to my community and engaging in community service has always made my heart feel complete, ever since I served my church and school as a young girl. Soon, I felt a strong calling to represent the needs of veterans.

COMMUNITY WARRIOR

I ended up staying at A Safe Haven for about four months, a little longer than some. Eventually, however, A Safe Haven and the VA helped me find a place to live and it was then that I continued to volunteer in the community, especially for veterans.

With contacts I made from church, I began serving at wellness events for veterans and organized events that concentrated on mitigating stress and PTSD. I founded an initiative called My Mind Matters that outlines the benefits to seeking mental health support and how it affects our lives in so many ways. The mental health summit hosted 170,000 viewers all over the world. I also received a fellowship to attend Warrior Summit. One day, someone told me that because of my passion and varied experiences that I should serve in public office. Now, I'm seriously considering it!

Also, I am the founder of Veteran One Stop Shop, LLC. Our company strives to provide excellent services in training, practical guides, one-on-one mentorship, and step-by-step goals to help others uncover the destination that they have for their business. I have seen a common thread among entrepreneurs—a lack of proper business development and residual strategy. Most companies know how to establish passive income and design their business to appeal to their customer, but they lack the courage to admit that there are some business processes that are unfamiliar to them or unique to their particular needs. Our goal is to be a transitional hub for entrepreneurial veterans, within the business community.

Our company carries many facets of expertise and experience, but ultimately, we help businesses reach their highest goals. We provide assistance with legal structure, ascertaining government contracts, business grants, startup residual strategy, and overall back office development. We focus on the business aspects that customers don't see. This work has become a passion for me, as I serve and help other veterans launch their businesses.

Today, my child continues to do well in school and aspires to accomplish great things in our community too. While we both have many roads to recover and repair, A Safe Haven provided the stabilization we needed to kick-start our freedom and security. Thank you again, A Safe Haven!

In gratitude, I continue to volunteer my time to A Safe Haven whenever possible. Most recently I have also helped and participated in daily debriefings online and brought awareness to A Safe Haven during the COVID-19 pandemic. I was pleased to see the organization gaining awareness and recognition for opening the first COVID-19 positive isolation space for the homeless in the City of Chicago. It is a remarkable contribution to our most vulnerable who need a place to go after testing positive for COVID-19.

I am grateful for A Safe Haven's staff and leaders, and all they did for me when I needed them most. Thanks to them, I am currently in stable housing and building the Veteran One Stop Shop. I also hope to advocate for better benefits for mothers who have been discharged from the military.

Throughout my experiences before, during, and after A Safe Haven, I have lost, I have learned, and I have gained. I know my story is not over and that I still have many things to accomplish. My experience at A Safe Haven was amazing, and I know I would not be where I am without their help. As a result, I am now able to rebuild a better tomorrow for my legacy. My goals are expanding as a result of a bright future! The sky has no limit just like my future!

Thank you, A Safe Haven family!

FINAL THOUGHTS

As military personnel transition into civilian life, I believe there are two main concerns regarding veterans benefits as they relate to the U.S. Housing & Urban Development-Veterans Affairs Supportive Housing (HUD-VASH): their scope of support and their accessibility.

HUD-VASH voucher programs should extend to the children of veterans. Transition to military life is mentally challenging enough. We should not also put our veterans through a tough emotional and financial transition by separating them from their immediate family because the HUD-VASH program does not support the family unit as a whole. It only makes sense that a single mother veteran, whose child was born while the mother was in service, will need support for her child as well as herself after discharge. For me, the military was my family who supported me for years. After my honorable discharge, it was baffling to discover that transitional care was available for me, but not my child.

The other concern that I personally faced was the inaccessibility of my benefits. The amount of bureaucracy (a.k.a. red tape) surrounding the receipt of benefits after discharge is unacceptable. A streamlined process should be evaluated and implemented. Because of my relocations for my personal safety, I had to start over with the VA in whatever state I was living in at the time. There was no communication between VA offices, or an apparent way to streamline the process. As a result, I suffered emotionally and financially because of this gap in service, and I will continue to advocate for collaborative processes and improved procedures surrounding veterans' benefits, until nobody else will ever have to experience what I went through.

After fleeing a life-threatening domestic abuse situation with her child, honorably discharged veteran Nikelcia Marcelin endured a downward struggle of denied veterans benefits, PTSD, identity theft, and homelessness before finding peace and security at A Safe Haven. Today she runs her own business, Veterans One Stop Shop, and is active in the community.

ROBERT HOVEY

"Without the supportive structure that A Safe Haven gave me,
I could never stay on the beam by myself."

Graduating Class: 2001
Length of Stay: 17 months
Current Status: President & CEO of a Sales and Marketing Company
Vice President and Partner of a Motion Picture Company

SWEET SURRENDER

Even when your circumstances in life or bad decisions lead you to dark places you never expected to go, it's nice to know there is still a way out. In my case, I found that the key to finding the way out was to surrender.

FINDING DIRECTION

I grew up in Skokie, Illinois with two younger brothers. We were the sons of a fireman in Wilmette, who later became the fire chief. When I was four years old, my dad and mom got divorced, and I never saw or heard from my real mother again.

Our dad remarried a couple years later, but before that happened, all three of us had lived with different people and rarely saw each other. My new stepmom took on the difficult task of raising three boys. Although she was a stay-at-home mother, she wasn't very loving, and my father seemed to always be at work. I was left feeling empty and looking for attention in order to feel loved. Also, I didn't get along with my stepmother, which didn't help.

When I was twelve, she left us for several months, claiming we were all too difficult for her. She did this by leaving three Valentine's Day cards for us to open that each said good-bye.

During my teenage years, I was a B and C student, caring more about art and music than academics. I had been a drummer since I was four years old and had won several state and national competitions throughout my childhood. In high school, I remember drinking alcohol a few times, but I only experimented with marijuana once.

When I turned seventeen, I joined the Marines and quickly excelled in the Marine Band. Then, after I was honorably discharged, I moved to Las Vegas and met a girl. When I was twenty-one, we got married, and it was then that my life of drug abuse began.

ENTER ADDICTION

My wife was from Los Angeles and involved in the Hollywood glam rock scene, which I found extremely attractive. We dove in together, and before I knew it, our addiction to heroin consumed us in every aspect. At the time, I was working as a salesman and earning great money. I remember getting paychecks for thousands of dollars that all went to buy heroin. Often, we were so broke, we had no electricity.

I was also very spiritually and physically sick. I can remember owning a monkey, a pot belly pig, a blue and gold macaw, and a dog, but we had no running water because I didn't pay the bill and all I cared about was getting my next fix. Finally, my wife left me to go live with her parents in Florida and get clean. My idea was to get clean also and then go join her, but the universe had other plans.

I quickly spiraled even further into the depths of addiction and then became homeless, eating out of dumpsters, and sleeping outside under a bridge by the railroad tracks in downtown Las Vegas. I felt out of control and desperate for help. I had once thought of getting clean but now it felt like it was far beyond my power to do so.

One night, when I really felt I could not go on and I was desperate for help, I looked up at the stars and prayed to a God that I hoped existed, even though I had no relationship with him. I asked to be rescued from my living situation, because I didn't know what else I could do.

The very next day, after meeting someone at a transient hotel, I was stabbed from behind in the side of the face. When I passed out, someone threw me out of a fourth story hotel window. I woke up in the trauma unit and had 176 stitches in my head, a broken chin, orbital rim, nose, and four vertebrae. I had shrunk two inches from the impact and weighed only 156 pounds in a full body cast.

DIFFERENT THIS TIME

For the next few months, I returned home to Chicago to recuperate at my dad's house. I hadn't spoken to him in a couple of years because of the shame I felt for who I had become. My dad had since remarried, and once I had physically recovered, my addiction resurfaced. My new stepmother asked me to find other living arrangements and I was on my own again.

I moved from one job to another, feeding my addiction to heroin and now crack cocaine. I became homeless again, this time in Chicago. I would shack up in abandon houses on the west side. Eventually, I was arrested and thrown in jail for forging my boss's signature on some blank checks to fund my habit.

On the first day inside my cell, I dropped to my knees and prayed, once again. But this time was much different. Instead of asking God to get me out of my mess, I apologized for how I was living and the things I did. I only asked for strength to help me face whatever consequences I might be facing. And at the time, I was facing sixteen felony counts of forgery and many years behind bars. How was it possible that a suburban, middle-class, smart and decent looking young man was facing this horrible reality? I couldn't help thinking that none of this was supposed to happen. I wasn't raised this way, and I certainly had much bigger dreams for myself.

Through a series of fortunate events, which I attribute all to God once I became willing to truly surrender to Him, I was bailed out. I found a great attorney to represent me who had compassion for my struggle, and I was able to secure residence at A Safe Haven in Chicago. I couldn't believe that I was actually given a key to the front door of an apartment that I could call home. I was so grateful and lucky to be alive that it showed in everything I did. I got one of my old jobs back and after a couple years, I was even made a partner.

I learned how to live without drugs, but even more importantly, how to be a good person with character and integrity. Without the supportive structure that A Safe Haven gave me, I could never stay on the beam by myself.

BUILDING A BETTER LIFE

While living at A Safe Haven, another friend and neighbor of mine from there introduced me to Melissa. They had been roommates at A Safe Haven, but my friend had since moved out and was still playing on the alumni softball team.

Melissa and I dated for a year and a half and then decided to get married. Five years later, we had twin girls, Grace and Olivia. When the girls were about seven years old, Melissa and I made the big leap to both leave our high-paying, secure jobs and follow our entrepreneurial spirit by opening up a sales and marketing company.

With a lot of hard work and talent, it took off like a storm and quickly grew to fifty employees. We did very little to no advertising to recruit people to work with us, but we instead relied primarily on word of mouth in the recovery community to give those who needed a second chance the opportunity to have an incredible job. Our company works with many recovery homes, including A Safe Haven, to provide employment. When needed, some of these recovery homes provide housing for our employees.

Although Melissa and I are no longer married, we have maintained an amicable relationship, enjoy parenting our two beautiful children, and continue to reap the rewards of our company. Melissa has been sober twenty-two years, and I had eighteen years until a brief relapse. But now, after surrendering again, I'm almost a year sober.

Today, our business employs several successful people in recovery that make six figures, and every month we take a day off to donate our time and resources to volunteer at local charities. One of our best employees, who was awarded our trophy for Outstanding Performance in 2020, is a former resident of A Safe Haven. She started with us while she was there and just moved out on her own a few months ago. She has added so much to our organization, while being a positive force among our other employees, and that's invaluable to us. The life skills and support that A Safe Haven provides are vital to creating a solution to the problem of today's growing recovery community.

Melissa and I are both personally indebted and most grateful to the miraculous organization that Neli and Brian Rowland built. We are true advocates for A Safe Haven and committed to helping however we can. Recovery has taught us to give back and always pay it forward. This never stops and is the essence of us staying alive and well. A Safe Haven taught us how to be that way in our business life, as well as our personal ones. Thank you, Neli, for creating such a place in this world.

FINAL THOUGHTS

Without A Safe Haven helping me when I needed it most, I would either be dead or in jail today. It is without question that A Safe Haven should be given all funding and resources available to help it grow and support the thousands of people that are in crisis mode.

Having dealt with different treatment centers, recovery homes, and been homeless and in jail myself, I am uniquely qualified from both ends of the spectrum to see what works and what doesn't. A Safe Haven has a winning model that could and should be replicated at other metropolitan areas across the country! Support them today!

After battling substance abuse for more than a decade and surviving homelessness and prison, Robert is now living in sobriety as a loving father of two daughters and operates his own sales and marketing company.

AUTHOR BIOGRAPHY

Neli Vazquez Rowland hails from one of Chicago's immigrant communities called 'Little Village'. Today she is an influential force and a passionate advocate for the homeless. In 1994, Neli and her husband Brian launched A Safe Haven to address and heal the root causes of the growing opioid and homeless epidemics. Now, the organization is frequently lauded as one of the most successful, vertically-integrated delivery systems and continuum of care models that provides people access to transitional housing, and individualized social services, including job training and placement and supportive and permanent affordable housing. A Safe Haven has helped 130,000 people transform their lives to short and long-term independence and self-sufficiency. Her authentic, courageous, and visionary approach to confronting and solving one of America's most challenging issues has made her a highly sought-after speaker by top media, academia, and local, national, and international public policy stages. She is an award-winning humanitarian and entrepreneur, a co-author of landmark State legislation, and the co-creator of Chicago's first COVID-19 Medical Respite center serving vulnerable populations in need of a place to isolate. Neli also serves on various business association, academic, healthcare, and governmental boards. She is also the author of An Elegant Solution, her memoir about building A Safe Haven, and the book HEALING, an anthology of personal success stories told by alumni of A Safe Haven. Both were published in 2021.

Neli is married to her husband and ASH co-founder Brian Rowland and the mother of two sons, Devin, and Dylan. She is also passionate about physical fitness and believes it helps reduce stress and improve your mental health and creativity. She is an avid runner, 2-time marathon finisher, multiple triathlete finisher and the producer of Chicago's oldest, largest, and now first ever Global Virtual Run/Walk to End Homelessness.

Contact: Neli@ASafeHaven.org
LinkedIn: www.linkedin.com/in/nelivazquezrowland

ASAFEHAVEN®
Housing is Healthcare®

A Safe Haven Foundation is a 501(c)3 not for profit, social enterprise that helps people aspire, transform and sustain their lives as they transition from homelessness to self-sufficiency with pride and purpose. A Safe Haven provides the tools for each individual to overcome the root causes of homelessness through a holistic and scalable model. A Safe Haven's visible social and economic impact unites families, stabilizes neighborhoods, and creates vibrant, viable communities.

100% of the proceeds from every sale of this book goes directly to help the homeless at A Safe Haven. Thank you for supporting our mission. ASHF is a not for profit 501(c)3. All donations are tax deductible to the fullest extent of the law. A Safe Haven Foundation Tax ID #36-4444200.

Learn More or Donate Today: **www.ASafeHaven.org**

IF YOU LOVED HEALING, READ THE INSPIRATION BEHIND BUILDING A SAFE HAVEN, AS TOLD BY THE CO-FOUNDER

With the head of a businesswoman and the heart of a warrior, Neli Vazquez Rowland burrows headlong into the intertwined challenges of substance abuse and homelessness on the streets of Chicago. While building the elegant solution known as A Safe Haven, she holds a mirror to our broken systems, decades before the world saw them as broken, and goes "all in" to challenge the status quo.

After overcoming personal challenges within their own lives, Neli and her husband, Brian are joined by like-minded citizens to sound the alarm of the growing opioid and homeless epidemics. Neli disrupts her life and steps out of her comfort zone to help herald a holistic, systematic approach to deliver the services individuals need to lift themselves off the streets and into self-sufficiency with pride and purpose.

Peppered with personal and professional stories of setbacks and triumph, *An Elegant Solution* chronicles the building of a powerful "proof of concept" that invites the private and public sectors to think differently and to join forces focused on building a more compassionate, productive, and positive response to America's most societal challenges—homelessness, the opioid crisis, and COVID-19.

NOW AVAILABLE ON AMAZON.COM

2750 West Roosevelt Road Chicago, IL, 60608

Phone: (773) 435-8300

Email: info@asafehaven.org